7 years on the road

7 years on the road

7 years on the road

An Outward and Inner Journey

7 years on the road

By the same author

The Rig Veda
New Complete Complete English Translation

The 7 Rivers Civilization
Sapta Sindhu: the civilization without ego

7 years on the road

7 years on the road

© 2025 HERVÉ LE BÉVILLON
EDITION: BOD · BOOKS ON DEMAND, 31 AVE NUE SAINT-RÉMY, 57600 FORBACH, BOD@BOD.FR
PRINTING: LIBRI PLUREOS GMBH, FRIEDENSALLEE 273, 22763 HAMBURG (GERMANY)
PRINT ON DEMAND
ISBN: 978-2-3226-1372-4
LEGAL DEPOSIT: MAY 2025

7 years on the road

An Outward and Inner Journey

Hervé Le Bévillon

7 years on the road

> I dreamed, I saw Joe Hill last night
> Alive as you and me
> Says I "But Joe, you're ten years dead"
> "I never died" says he
> "I never died" says he
> ......
>
> Joan Baez

to all my Joe Hill

All illustrations are royalty-free and come from
https://commons.wikimedia.org/ ;
https://creativecommons.org/publicdomain/zero/1.0/

7 years on the road

November 2024

I just turned off the TV. I'm still in shock. No, I wasn't dreaming, I definitely saw the flooded Sahara! There are even lakes! Rivers and lakes! And, what's more, that's where I drove! The dunes, where the trucks that got stuck in the sand had to be pulled out, are flooded... And further south, the Zinder mosque collapsed. It was made of earth, like all those in the Sahel, since it almost never rains.

We're living in a wonderful time, as Reiser[1] said. This year in Delhi, it was so hot that fifteen election workers died of heat! Two or three years ago, birds were dying in flight, also in Delhi! That year, in Lokarn, my village in the heart of central Brittany, it was 42 degrees, while on the same day, at the same time, it was only 37 degrees in Agadez and Delhi. And it was almost spring in Bangui, with only 27 degrees.

Global temperatures are rising every year. Water wars have already begun, and many more are brewing, for water and other resources vital to our modern world.

And, meanwhile, world leaders still think they're in the 19th century, with wars fought over territories, borders, or other dubious reasons. The pride and vanity of the "great" of this world remains the same. Obsessed with their own image, they see nothing coming...

Time flies, and I've been able to see the evolution of our lives, we little whites.

When I was a kid, women would throw themselves on the horse dung left behind by those who pulled the hearses. It was excellent fertilizer for flower pots.

In the evenings, we watched the radio. More precisely, we listened to the radio while watching it. Television was commercially available the year I was born, but it took a while for ordinary people to buy it. We walked to school, regardless of the weather.

---
[1] a French humorist

7 years on the road

Now everything has changed, including mentalities. Of course, it's better, in terms of comfort. No need to fetch water from the well, no more gray coats, but computers, smartphones, etc. But other problems have arisen. There are more than eight billion of us on Earth. The temperature rises every year. This causes disruptions and unexpected natural disasters, such as, for example, monstrous floods in Pakistan and, less serious but surprising, snow in Saudi Arabia.

The world has completely changed before my eyes. That's the advantage of being old. You see the evolution of life and thought, and unfortunately, it's getting worse.

But it's good to be old. Not so good for the body, because it breaks down like all old mechanical things. On the other hand, for the mind, it's excellent.
Among other things, we revisit the moments that mattered most in our lives, before globalization.

For me, it started when I was about to turn twenty...

On the road. 1967-1968

September 1967. I was about to turn twenty when I left as a "beatnik." I hadn't read Kerouac, Burroughs, or the others, but it was really in the air. I was working in a post-synchronization studio in Paris. It was a scam. I started at the beginning of July and finished at the end of August. The boss did the same thing every year. Rather than hiring an extra to replace his projectionist on vacation, he brought a young candidate for the job up from the "deep provinces" in July, extended the trial period in early August, under the pretext that there wasn't much work, dangling the dream life in front of him, and on August 16, he told him he wasn't keeping him on. I only found out after meeting an old projectionist, while looking for another job, in the Latin Quarter.

***

We're under De Gaulle. Women have only recently been allowed to wear trousers, and even then, not officially. They can't open a bank account without their husband's consent. They have no rights over their children; it's the father who has to sign and decide. They've had the right to vote for 23 years. Three years before I was born!

The age of majority is 21. So I'm still a minor. The atmosphere is heavy and oppressive in this Gaullist France. The churches are still full. In Brittany, my country, women go to mass on Sunday mornings and men go to the chapel. That is, to the pub. The streets are empty.

The ultimate dishonor for a man was to have long hair. That is, at the time, practically anything longer than a crew cut. The joke among aggressive, drunken proles was: Is your hairdresser on strike?

Homosexuality sends quite a few people to prison. In short, France before 1968 was far from joyfull. Racism was very common. Even though it wasn't the case at my parents' house at all, everyone considered Arabs and blacks to be almost human. It's not mean, it's just how it is: on one side there are the superior whites—especially the French and the English, convinced they invented everything in terms of humanism and civilization—and on the other side, anyone who was more or less tanned.

The white man's duty is to civilize inferior peoples. And among these whites, the French are by far the most open to human rights. In any case, they are truly convinced of it. What they forget to say is that these are the rights of white men only, and preferably Parisians. That's how it is, practically everyone shares this vision of things. On the right as on the left. Especially on the right. On the left for the good of the inferior man, even if it means imposing happiness on him with bayonets. The right is more venal but hides behind the values of the Christian West, of course. And yet the Algerian War has been over for five years, Africa has been decolonized, but that doesn't change anything, the average Frenchman remains convinced of being superior. It's in his DNA.

We are raised on the myth of the French Resistance, almost silently mentioning the fact that its official policy was collaboration with Nazi Germany. The French police are in the spotlight. There is barely any mention of their Vel d'Hiv roundup and the hunts for Jews and resistance fighters, which they carried out right up un til the eve of the liberation of Paris. The values of this era are practically those of Pétain: Work, Family, Fatherland. There is no arguing, no protesting, it's not done. Period. The one who is right is the leader or the one wearing a tie.

This life doesn't appeal to me. Not at all. My adolescence was ruined by school, which I was bored to tears. It didn't interest me. School bored me considerably. I had absolutely no ambition and didn't see myself at all in the future. I took refuge in the quasi-religious listening of rock 'n' roll, with Gene Vincent, for the music, and I became politicized with Léo Ferré[1], for the lyrics.

I still ended up getting a BEPC[2] and a CAP[3] as a projection operator. And now I'm getting ripped off at my second job. I had worked for six months in a cinema in Brittany, in Rennes, just before.

---

[1] A famous Anarchist singer.
[2] Diploma for 12-year-olds.
[3] Professional qualification certificate.

7 years on the road

The life that lies ahead for me doesn't interest me at all. I want to see the world. Above all, I want to meet people who are different from the average Frenchman, to leave this sad and narrow-minded France. I feel I have to find something. My own life. Me, quite simply. I have to get rid of all the nonsense that was stuffed into my head during my youth. I have no desire to have a "good job," nor a bad one either, for that matter. I absolutely do not want to become a doctor or a teacher, any more than I want to be mayor or even rich.
Something else awaits me, I don't know what, but I'm dying to stay living in this gray and mean France before 1968, to get married, to have kids, to build a house and wait for retirement. It's grim.

Towards the end of August, while my notice period was still running, I spent the evenings on the stairs of Montmartre, without really understanding what these people from all over the world were doing, sitting on the steps, except that they traveled a lot and were happy to be together.

I've heard of beatniks before, but not yet hippies. They probably talked about them a bit on TV, but at that time, not everyone had a TV, especially not twenty-year-olds. Of course, there were the Beatles, Antoine[1] and his Ramblings[2], but that didn't reach many people outside of Paris and the privileged circles of the big "provincial" cities. From time to time, I see daddy's boys in flowered shirts with a daisy in their long hair. They're very clean. They try to copy the Americans and talk about peace and love, without their country being at war. For me, they're snobs and that doesn't appeal to me at all. On the other hand, what interests me most is dealing with non-French speakers.

At first, I had a little trouble with English, but I managed to make myself more or less understood. I wasn't too bad at it at school, despite the almost uninterrupted succession of teachers who were completely incompetent in pedagogy. They taught us English in French! I compensated by listening to rock 'n' roll classics. In the 10th grade, my English teacher asked me, seriously, if I had been raised in the USA. I would have liked that...

One evening, I brought a dozen people into my furnished room who didn't know where to sleep. Among them, a tall, thin man was a fan of a drug: amphetamines,

---

[1] First French singer with long hair.
[2] One of his famous songs

used for particularly difficult alcohol detoxification. It was also the secret behind the cycling exploits of the time. It was also what would kill Tom Simpson in the Tour de France that same year.

He offers me an injection and I accept. I haven't even smoked a joint in my life and I'm about to go straight to the big leagues, with a uncertain life expectancy. I'm ready, tourniquet in place, veins bulging. Ready to commit the biggest stupidity of my life. And at the precise moment the tall, skinny guy is about to stick his needle in my arm, someone knocks at the door. I take off my tourniquet and go to answer it. To my great surprise, it's Bernard, my childhood friend who had also been forced to go to work in Paris. I leave everyone behind, in my room, and go with him to tour the local bars. I'll never forget this disturbing coincidence. He unknowingly saved my life, or at the very least, he kept me from becoming a junkie. I'm convinced of it.

At the end of August, I'm heading to Amsterdam with a guy I met at the Sacré-Cœur. He's happy to introduce me to the road, probably also because I'm leaving with my last paycheck. I don't mind; I intend to blow it all as quickly as possible and be truly poor.

In fact, I didn't go to Holland, and instead stopped in Antwerp, where I hung around miserably at the Muse. It was a café, well-known among the small, marginal world that had been developing in recent years. It was owned by Turks and was occasionally frequented by Ferré Grignard, a star of the time.

After a few days, I was deported along with about ten other French nationals. It was an opportunity to discover the joys of police custody and my first experience of prison, since the deportation would take two days. We spent the night in Moons's cells. Seven of us slept in a room with three bunk beds. So they put mattresses on the floor for us.

Barely back in Paris, I hang out at Popov's on Rue de la Huchette in Saint-Michel, where you can spend the day in front of a small red wine for 30 centimes. He's a White Russian of about 70 who runs his bar with his daughter. All the backpackers passing through Paris come to drop off their backpacks in the back room. The cops arrive up to four times a day to check papers. Luckily, a cop from the police station warns Popov beforehand, which gives us time to get organized.

7 years on the road

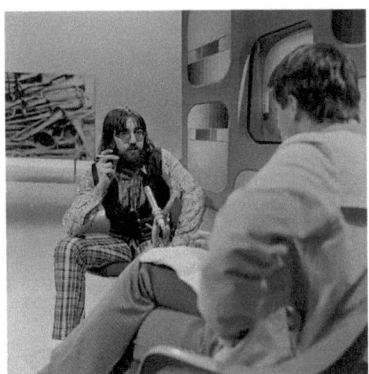

Ferré Grignard

It was the era of the eccentrics in Saint-Michel and Saint-Germain: There was especially André Dupont, known as Aguigui Mouna. Mouna was a former restaurateur, who publishes a newspaper sold at auction by beatniks and penniless students, they receive a percentage of the sales.

Mouna

7 years on the road

There was a difference between travelers and those who stayed put. They were called zonards[1], with a touch of contempt. The zonards spent their time looking for money. Living in Paris without working must have been a problem.

One day, a vague, slightly odd friend asked me to accompany him to Simone de Beauvoir's house, where JP Sartre was also. The friend had come to demand some money that Sartre owed him. They didn't seem to agree, and Sartre seemed quite annoyed. Finally, he asked me to help the friend out, who was in a rather strange state. He gave him a 100-franc note, taken from his outer jacket pocket, which was resting on the back of a chair, to help him get out. It was the first time I'd seen someone put their bills in that kind of pocket. It must have been small change for him.

Life is hard in Paris, penniless and without knowing anyone. At night, I walk for hours in Les Halles, and when the Métro[2] opens, I rush out before the ticket collector starts working. And I sleep on a bench in a quiet station. Other times, I go up to the top floor of a building[3] and sleep on the landing. All this, of course, without a sleeping bag or anything else.

JP Sartre

---

[1] A kind of slacker.
[2] The subway.
[3] There were no intercoms back then, you had to shout a name in front of the caretaker's lodge.

7 years on the road

I do a bit of begging, but I hate it and I stop as soon as I have enough money to buy a baguette. On lucky days, I buy a Tunisian sandwich, a real treat. But I don't like this life at all, so I quickly decide to hit the road again.
At first, I hitchhiked, usually with a guitar, through France, Italy, Switzerland, and Belgium. I only knew a few chords and was incapable of really tuning it properly, but it was part of the folklore, even if I annoyed many people.

Before leaving, I had bought a backpack and a sleeping bag. I had found them at the Saint-Ouen flea market. There was a strange atmosphere. All the vendors were huddled around the radios, looking serious, but I couldn't hear what was going on. Much later, I learned that it was the Six-Day War between Israel and the Arab countries.

A sleeping bag is comfortable and a little bulky, but in Europe, it's essential. One of the first nights, I was in the middle of the countryside somewhere in France. It wasn't raining, and I decided to sleep in a field, or rather a meadow, right next to the road. In the middle of the night, while I was sleeping soundly, I felt something like breathing next to my head. Since it couldn't be a girlfriend, I looked over and discovered a horse who must be wondering what I could be. Our story ends there, because he leaves. And I go back to sleep, very happy with this encounter.

I have a lot of adventures with the people who pick me up. They range from the guy who can't drive and who obviously has mental health problems—luckily the cops stop him before we kill each other—to the completely drunk grandpa who goes from Nice to Paris to shoot his son-in-law. He shows me his pistol and the loaded magazine in his glove compartment.

I wander around a bit everywhere: in Paris, Bordeaux, Dijon, Rome, Positano, Neuchâtel... When I like a place, I stay, and when I don't like it anymore, I leave. I get to know the night shelters, municipal or religious. There I meet lots of tramps and former legionnaires who were really shaken by the Algerian War.

In one of these shelters, I discover a business that one of the tramps has developed: he peels an orange and sells each slice to his colleagues for 10 cents. He should have thought of that!

7 years on the road

I'm a beginner, I don't know anything. I don't know the good spots, the places where I'm going to find nice people. I get stopped by the cops—or gendarmes—all the time when I'm hitchhiking. They call the central database to see if I'm wanted.

I commit petty thefts from time to time reluctantly, depending on the friends I have. I don't like stealing, but I get carried away sometimes. The thefts in question are still very rare and very pathetic. Like Camembert in a grocery store, fake hashish scam using Kub bouillon, fake LSD scam on blotter paper, etc. I leave my fingerprints and photos at more than one police station. Routine.

The big joke the cops tell us when we arrive at the police station for an identity check is: "I can't wait until next year when we get lawnmowers."

Sometimes I meet colleagues who are as disheveled as I am. Over a joint, we tell each other about our "adventures." Istanbul always comes up as a heavenly place.

In Marseille, I make a friend: Claude. He sings his own songs while accompanying himself on the guitar. We squat in a large building on Boulevard de Strasbourg with about ten other backpackers. One day, Claude and I decide to leave for Istanbul. But we have a problem: his clothes are at the dry cleaners and he doesn't have a penny to get them back. So he comes up with a brilliant idea: we're going to steal a car stereo from a car and resell it on Rue des Chapeliers where a small thieves' fair is being held, tolerated by the police.

Personally, I don't like it at all. No, it's not a question of morality—I refer to Proudhon[1] for his phrase "property is theft" in these cases—but the fear of getting caught. But, I'm going anyway. Stupidly.
No surprise, a patrol car catches us in the act. The loot is impressive: a blanket, a bungee cord, a pair of gloves, and a screwdriver. Pathetic thieves, pathetic loot, but a decent punishment: three months in prison. Not bad for beginners! We didn't even have a lawyer! I wouldn't see Claude again until the day of our release. He didn't linger; he went back to his parents' house. In Marseille!

---

[1] A famous French anarchist.

I should have been suspicious: a backpacker who puts his things in the dry cleaners!!!

The Baumettes

You have to love prison. Okay, we get food and shelter, but there are three of us to a cell 23 hours a day. And honestly, most of the young inmates are really stupid. Very stupid. And boastful. They're all Al Capones. None of them got caught by the cops, they were all "given away." They all talk about killing the guy who ratted them out.

In my first cell, I encounter two super gangsters my age who have different ideas about the honor of the underworld. One extols the virtues of pimping, and the other the morality of robbers. In reality, the first was convicted of rape, and the super-robber, of car theft, like me. Discussions about the morality of robbers and pimps quickly bore me.

Fortunately, the trial comes quickly. Claude and I take our three months in five minutes. It must be said that there are a lot of people, and without a lawyer, whom we had requested, things go faster.

7 years on the road

The advantage is that I get to change cells when I get back. This time the two occupants, also my age, are tough guys. The younger one was "beating up some faggot" in the public restrooms and the other had tried to settle a dispute with his boss with a crowbar one evening when he'd taken the pastis a bit too far.

My roommates have developed a system to designate who is on duty each week to clean the floor and toilets[1]. We play poker with matches and the loser is on duty. At first, I agree, but strangely, I always lose. I point this out, but it doesn't go down well. I feel that things are going to get worse. I prefer to ask the prison director to move me to another cell. I write to him and I don't have to wait long. He receives me with a big smile and tells me that I'm going to be happy: he's put me with anti-militarists!

Indeed, I like it. But only relatively. There are probably different categories of anti-militarists. These two guys are more of the moron type. The first is here for beating up a lieutenant one day when he was really drunk. The other for desertion. Not in the Boris Vian[2] style, but more like a sensitive little thug who wants to go back to his mother's. They do push-ups all day between combing their hair.

One new feature, though, is the opportunity to work in a workshop, just to keep busy and earn some money when we leave. We file the burrs off miniature cars coming out of the molds. We're paid by the piece. By the bag, to be exact. Every one has ten minutes to smoke a cigarette. The guard on duty isn't at all mean.
There are some bizarre rumors going around. One of them says that Donovan, while singing "Mellow Yellow," encourages us to smoke dried banana peels. The effect is said to be the same as hashish. Very stupidly, I spread some peels out to dry in the sun on the windowsill and smoked them. Of course, it didn't do any good. It was just ridiculous.

And then one day, news reached us. We could no longer bring in newspapers or magazines. We found that strange. Two days later, another, much more unpleasant news: we could no longer order tobacco. Fortunately, the two "anti-militarists" kept all their cigarette butts in a tin can.

---

[1] The word is a bit pompous.
[2] Famous French poet who wrote a song in which he refuses to go to war and kill people like himself.

7 years on the road

A few days later, we finally ask the workshop supervisor what's going on. "Nothing, there's just an unlimited general strike." He calls it nothing! It's the middle of May 1968[1]!

Even the best things must come to an end, they say. I'm leaving at the beginning of June. After seeing my friends from Marseille again, I hitchhike back to Paris. In Auxerre, I'm stuck for three days on the outskirts of the city. The locals look at me askance. There are posters everywhere showing protesters cutting down Parisian plane trees to put them on the barricades. In large letters, they read: "It's not by cutting down the trees that we reap the fruits."

Finally, after three days, I take off. I arrive in Paris and go to the banks of the Seine. At Saint-Michel, there are several CRS[2] trucks. A group of cheerful students goes to meet them. One of them tells me to join them; they're going to read poetry. I'm not interested, and I decline the invitation. Sitting on my sleeping bag, I intensely appreciate freedom. I realize that the word I love most in the French language is precisely that: freedom. It feels so good to discover it.

It was also the time of Michel Corringe who sang "la route[3]".

> *Oh, sure, I'm often hungry and cold*
> *I feel like stopping sometimes*
> *But the road still carries me away*
> *Desire to realize a symbol*
> *To possess the unique beauty*
> *That we call Liberty.*

---

[1] Famous revolt of young people against the established order.
[2] Riot police.
[3] The road

7 years on the road

7 years on the road

Sahara, here we come.

A few months later, after spending a week or two visiting my parents, who now understood my point of view – even if my father had to force himself a little – I decided to go to Africa.

I had been hanging around Rennes for a bit, where I had made some friends. There was no hashish, so we used over-the-counter products from pharmacies. It wasn't particularly good, but it allowed me to make four "abstract" drawings, since I have no talent. I had been struck by the Parisian fine arts students, who were making "chalks[1]" on the sidewalks. I told myself that it was a good way to survive. I kept them carefully for a long time. They were awful, but hey, it was better than nothing.

Leaving for Algeria has nothing to do with leaving for Istanbul, but I want to discover the world, to leave Europe. I'm fed up with police checks, with rednecks who call us all sorts of names, because we have long hair[2]. I want to see something else, other people, other cultures. In my passport, I have a 100 franc note that my mother gave me on the sly before I left.
With that, I just have enough to take the boat from Marseille to Skikda.

The boat is packed with Algerians returning home. Arriving at the port, in the large disembarkation hall, I see a queue of several hundred passengers who have to declare the money they are bringing to their families. I'm very embarrassed because I don't have a cent and I have no desire to wait in line.

A little to one side, a big, smiling policeman in uniform, rifle slung over his shoulder, oversees the smooth running of the formalities with a certain benevo-

---
[1]Colored chalk drawings.
[2]Mine aren't growing, but my beard is.

lence. I go to see him and explain that I have no money. He's nice, and he takes me through customs without making a declaration.

I'm amazed. French cops could use a lesson. And then I find myself outside. The weather is beautiful, even though it's winter. It was snowing in Marseille before I left.

I head towards Constantine and stick out my thumb. Three cars immediately stop. I've never seen anything like it! Not wanting to offend anyone, I hesitate a little, but finally, I take the first one that stops.

In Constantine, I decide to exhibit my drawings in a fairly large square. A crowd of young people gathers and I chat with them. They give me what they can while I finish writing a magnificent "help me continue my journey" in full color. That's the only thing that's more or less beautiful in what I'm exhibiting. But, I don't have time to finish, two cops arrive and tell me to pick up my things and get out. Which I do without any particular emotion. This isn't the first time I've been kicked out.

I don't have time to go far because the young people are practically jostling to invite me into their homes. They explain to me that it is a duty for Muslims to help travelers. I spend several days going from one family to another. I see everyone, cousins, uncles, grandparents... Everywhere the welcome is wonderful. I still regret, inwardly of course, seeing practically only men. The women are a little too discreet.

I'm also discovering the meaning of burping. My father, who spent eight years in Morocco in the "colonial" army, told me that it was polite to burp after a good meal. In fact, it means: "I've eaten enough, thank God." So, the families who host me feed me until I burp naturally. I finally understand, on the verge of indigestion. I should have faked it!

One thing that interests me a lot is their perception of the Algerian War. They talk to me about it without any problem and I notice that they don't hold it against the "roumis[1]", despite what we did to them. There is no resentment. They are mainly interested in France. Their dream is to go and live there. Those who return to

---

[1] The Romans.

their countries with the famous white 404[1] are considered heroes. They make no reference to the very real racism that existed at the time.

When I leave Constantine, I hitchhike again, and boom, two more cars brake sud denly. It's the perfect country for a hitchhiker!

Constantine

In Algiers, in front of the central post office, I meet a very nice German. His name is Rudy. He speaks French quite well. He's like me, that is to say: completely broke. He has a guitar. He's set off on the road without really knowing why. He lets himself be carried along by events. We spend a few days making "chalks" not far from the main post office. It goes very well. Even the beggars, including a blind man, are keen to give us something. We refuse, of course, but they insist heavily. We end up accepting, so as not to offend them.

We're spoiled for choice when it comes to accommodation. All the young people, usually students, invite us. Hospitality isn't legendary in Algeria. It must be very strange for them when they come to France.

One day, a show promoter asked Rudy to sing two or three songs as the opening act for a local artist. He was clever, because his songs weren't interesting to any-

---
[1] A car.

one, so he opened with traditional music, which filled the venue. He gave Rudy a little time right afterward. During intermission, before the local artist could perform, the venue emptied by more than half.

Rudy is tempted by crossing the Sahara. It suits me perfectly, and we leave Algiers and our friends for the adventure. He has some grass with him. We head towards Ghardaïa. Still hitchhiking. Our plan is super simple. We cross the entire desert to Tamanrasset and go to Agadez in Niger. After that, we'll see.

Ghardaia

We cross landscapes whose beauty is unimaginable. The images we had of them came from television, were rare and in black and white. We are not in the sand dunes, but in the desert of yellow stones and earth. We stop at a few palm groves and oases. It's very pleasant! Because the sun beats down hard, I become a fan of the turban, chèche, or chechia in Arabic.

The change of scenery is total. The truck drivers who transport us, for free I should add, are extremely friendly. This doesn't stop them from wondering why we're going into the desert, without any equipment, when we could be living peacefully in Europe, which they tend to confuse with paradise. The road takes us to the last town: Tamanrasset. The paved road ends there. This is where the convoys to Niger are organized. It is strictly forbidden to travel with a single vehicle across the desert. The locals tell us many tragic stories of Westerners who set off on an adventure without warning the Algerian police and were found dead of thirst near their broken-down cars.

It's very hot. We think we've probably forgotten something. A water bottle! Nothing much. A friendly cop we're chatting with offers us a one-liter bottle. Thanks, police, I'm not used to it.

Tamanrasset

A little later, he tells us that a convoy is forming with Westerners and that they are taking away anyone who asks them. Great!

The man organizing the crossing is Greek. He confirms that he wants us. No problem. He has a sizable convoy: three large semi-trailer trucks with a second trailer behind them, a bus, a cantonal type, and a small dump truck that looks like it's made for the desert. Each truck, except the small one, is loaded with used

7 years on the road

Mercedes cars destined for sale in Niger. The bus is destined for Nigeria, which happens to be in the midst of a civil war in Biafra.

We're not the only passengers. Besides the five German drivers, we have some nice people. Five or six French people, including a woman, three English people, two Americans, two Belgians, five Tuaregs, and three or four black Nigerians. We fraternize with the Tuaregs and the Blacks.

The two Belgians are friends who sold everything they had to fulfill a long-held dream: sailing around the world. Unfortunately, the boat sank right off the Canary Islands, and now they're heading to Biafra to enlist as mercenaries. The English are nice. They have a sense of humor that we like. Among the Americans, there's one who served in Vietnam. He tells the others about his adventures on the bus in the evening.
As you might have guessed, there's a divide within the group: on one side are the poor: the Blacks, the Tuaregs, and us. On the other side are everyone else, with a slight difference for the English.

On the day of departure, an Algerian officer gave us three loaves of bread and three cans of sardines. Enough to last the three-day journey. That's how long all convoys spend on the sandy track from Tamanrasset to Agadez. The Greek boasted that he knew the route and the shortcuts well. This worried me a little, even though he'd already made this trip.

It's time to go, let's go. Rudy and I settle into a Mercedes, inside the tarpaulin-covered truck. It's looking promising! Since the tarps aren't transparent, we might not see anything of the desert.

The VIPs bought themselves lots of treats to help them survive the trip (orange juice, chips, etc.). We made a deal with the Greek: we could drink from the water in stock whenever we needed it. There's just one small problem: it's hot, but hey, we're getting used to it.

In the evening, everyone goes down. We eat our bread and our sardines in oil. Someone, one of the German drivers, wrote "the animals wagen" in the dust covering the Tuaregs' and Nigerians' trucks.

Boris, one of the two Belgians, wants to take a little walk under the starry sky. A few of us go. We have no compass, no map, no guidebook, nothing at all. Boris, the Belgian, explains to us that we must take such and such a star as a marker, and on the way back, we will simply have to get back on track. Of course, when we return, the stars are no longer in the same place. But we find the convoy quite easily, nonetheless.

The night is quite cold. To sleep, we dig a bed in the sand, as the Tuaregs explained to us, and we fall asleep easily, unlike the whites who spent the night in the bus and trucks. In the morning we have tea with them and try to hold a conversation. We manage, thanks to gestures, the little Arabic we understand. There is even one who teaches me to write, in the sand, my name in Tamachek — the language of the Tuaregs —. It sounds like Unfortunately, the sounds are not the same in the two languages. The sounds Her and Vé in my first name do not exist, so I am learning to write Harfé.

A Targi, Tuaregs

We re-embark. On our way to Niger! But after the Algerian border post, the track disappears. And that's where it really begins. It can no longer be called a track. There are tire tracks going in all directions and large black barrels marking one, from time to time. Occasionally, we see the carcasses of cars, including a 2CV bent in two.

7 years on the road

The three large trucks and the bus keep getting stuck in the sand. Rudy and I immediately understand the reason for the Greek's "generosity." He needs people to carry the sheet metal from the side of the truck under its wheels. What a hassle! And yet, we're probably on the main track. The black barrels, though rare, confirm it. It's going to take more than three days, that's for sure. The Greek doesn't think to ask one of the Tuaregs to guide him. He will eventually do so, a few days later.

The good thing about being stuck in the sand is that we get out of our Mercedes and appreciate the scenery. Like any self-respecting ignoramus, I thought the desert was empty. It's stupid. There are lots of little bird footprints on the sand, tracks of small animals... And a minute after stopping, we find ourselves invaded by flies. We wonder where they come from.

It's the ballet of the sheet metal. They're heavy, but the Tuaregs and the Nigerians are happy to carry them alone at arm's length. And one afternoon, there's no way to get the semi-trailers out of the sand. We spend ages there, sweating, but no, nothing doing.

Finally, the Greek decides to wait until the next morning. The sand would be harder, and we should be able to get out. We want to believe it, but we no longer know where the track is. Finally, more fear than harm, the next morning, the trucks quickly get out of the sand, and we find the track again fairly quickly.

That's it, the trucks are freed from the sand for at least the fiftieth time, and we're speeding toward the Niger border post. And then, something rattles in the engine of the bus the VIPs are traveling in. This is serious; we have to get a part from Germany to Algiers, and then to Tamanrasset, and then to the Niger border. All this by plane to Tamanrasset, and then by Jeep! It's going to be expensive. Very expensive.

What to say, what to do? Nothing. And wait. Rudy and I meet the Nigerien soldiers. It's a joyful mess in their guard post. Automatic weapons hang by their shoulder straps from the ends of the beds, magazines loaded. They welcome us warmly and give us a piece of grilled gazelle leg to eat. It's delicious. While we're there, I ask the highest-ranking officer if he can give us something to satisfy our hunger for the coming days, because we have nothing left. He's very kind and gives us enough to eat for several days, plus some wood for cooking. We thank him and his men, and we go to feast.

Imagine the same thing, but with trucks and no uniforms.

Boris walks by us. He's surprised to see that we've been given something. He goes to find the post commander and comes back with a big smile. We finish the little grass Rudy finds in his bag. Lying in the sand, we admire the stars and the clear sky.

The night was good. But we're still stuck, because of that damn bus. And then, a Land Rover leaves the border post with two soldiers armed with assault rifles in the back. It's either war or hunting. It returns a few hours later with Boris, whom we hadn't noticed, smiling regally. He pulls a beautiful gazelle out of the back of the 4x4. Party with the VIPs tonight. Yes, and we won't be invited. In fact, we don't care.

It's one of the German drivers preparing the mechoui. A hunter, no doubt. Boris goes to see the commander. He comes back looking really angry. I think I guessed why. I'm all ears. From what he explains to the VIPs, the commander re fuses to give him wood because it's too rare in the desert. And what's more, he wants to charge for hunting, diesel, and ammunition. The English join us. They weren't invited either. To our great pleasure, we witness the preparation of the mechoui. A tire! They set fire to a tire and place the gazelle on top! Obviously, it becomes inedible, and the dirty black smoke coming out of the tire must be visible from several dozen kilometers away. And it stinks!

Despite everything, we still arrived in Agadez after ten days stuck in the sand and a wait of about three days at the border post. Rudy spoke with one of the German drivers.

Agadez

The Greek was buying used Mercedes cars and trucks. He placed an ad like this: "Drivers wanted for a free trip to Africa and a free return flight." They weren't very happy. But they arrived, and it will ultimately be a good memory for them. They told us that the Greek runs his trucks on domestic fuel, which is illegal everywhere.

We just find it a little curious that everything is being sold in Niger except the ab normally heavy bus that's supposed to go to Nigeria, in the middle of the Biafran

7 years on the road

War. Were there weapons inside, under the floorboards, whose screws holding the flooring together are too clean to be old? Its market value must have been significant to have a part flown in.

It should be noted, however, that the Greek had to give a Mercedes to one of the bosses of the Nigerian police to be able to continue to Niamey.

We are not staying in Agadez, but are going to Zinder where we are settling in for a few days.

In Niamey, Rudy and I part ways. He wants to continue west, and I want to stay a while. I love Africa! I love Africans!

One of the things that strikes me most is the kids who call me Boss. I can tell them I'm not one, but it doesn't change anything; for them, a white person is a boss.

Zinder

So, I exhibit my horrible drawings on the only sidewalk in town, the one in front of the Pariscoa store. I'm with the lepers and other beggars. They all call me

Boss, and in the end, I let it be. The first time I shook the hand—if I dare say so—of a leper, I felt a little apprehensive. And then, in the end, I didn't pay any more attention. I'm really discovering black Africa. I make a friend, a white technical aid worker. Nice, until the day he explains to me that in May '68, the French government should have hanged three demonstrators as an example.

One day, I was at the market and saw the army arrive, assault rifles in hand. They evacuated the market, forcing everyone—except me—to go to the side of the road to applaud a passing foreign minister. They distributed small flags in the colors of the said country, and everyone obeyed, then, once the procession had passed, the "volunteers" returned to their jobs. Organized spontaneity is beautiful!

The Pariscoa of Niamey 1972

A French couple, who came in a 404 that broke down upon arrival, hosts all the backpackers who pass through the area. They found work as soon as they arrived. They're chefs in an ice block factory. There are already about ten people living with them. I'm happy to see some backpackers again. There were quite a few people doing the loop: Algiers – Agadez – Niger – Upper Volta – Ivory Coast, and

7 years on the road

they were taking the boat back to Europe. They were traveling with a little money, of course.

We're discovering African grass. It's really good and costs almost nothing.
It's the community, as was common at the time: fifteen people living with someone who was the only one working. It usually ends badly. Here, the couple is on the verge of divorce and finally they throw everyone out. I continue alone towards Burkina Faso—called Upper Volta at the time.

It's a poor country, poorer than Niger, and I greatly appreciate the kindness of the people. Europe seems to me, more than ever, to be a zone of aggression, selfishness, stupidity, and meanness.

A little after the border post, I sit in the shade of a mango tree and notice that almost everyone is naked, with a few exceptions. My jeans are hot, so I change into my swimming trunks. Immediately, a cop yells at me, telling me we weren't at the beach here. Okay, no problem, but, well...

I arrive in a small village and since I have a little money on me, I decide to go have a beer. I enter a crowded bistro, and I am greeted by the screams of a baby a few months old, in his mother's arms. She is very embarrassed, smiles at me and tells me that it is the first time he sees a white person. I give her a big smile, and I tell her that at home it is the same thing. It is just the color that is not the same. She laughs too, and the baby calms down.

I spend a few days in Ouagadougou. I sleep in a solid building that must have been something more or less cultural. One day I meet an elderly woman. She's from Paimpol[1] who married a man from Upper Volta who dreams of becoming president of the republic. She compares her life to that of Angélique, Marquise of the Angels[2], and would like to write a book about it. I leave her to her dreams and decide to push on to Bobo-Dioulasso, thinking of heading towards West Africa.

Along the way, which I'm hitchhiking, as usual, but on the truckload since there are almost no cars, I stop in a village that prides itself on having sacred caimans.

---

[1] A port of Brittany.
[2] famous historical erotic movie.

7 years on the road

It's quite amusing to see people buy chickens from the villagers and throw them as close as possible to the caiman. Snap, a tiny bite, and the chicken is gone.

When the curious onlookers have left, while I stay there enjoying the shade of a mango tree[1], I see the village kids rushing towards the caimans and playing around them. I even see one climbing on the back of the biggest one. And every thing is going well. The kids are laughing, throwing themselves into the water while the monsters go and digest their chickens.

In Bobo-Dioulasso, I settle into a public garden that's a bit like a zoo. I spread my blanket[2] on a bench, not far from an orangutan very cramped in its small cage. I exhibit my drawings on the sidewalk of the local Pariscoa, and in the evening I treat myself to cafés au lait with salted margarine on toast. It's not Breton butter, but it's still good. And I love the atmosphere. I make lots of friends among the poorest of the poor. I discover modern African music. I'm happy and in my element. But I can't continue to West Africa, for political and warlike reasons beyond my control. The border is closed. I decide to return to Ouagadougou.

One evening, the truck that picked me up had to turn off and go in another direc tion. It dropped me off next to a house where everyone seemed to be asleep. Not wanting to disturb anyone, I settled down on the other side of the track and slept.

---

[1] I will often use this expression, but since I know nothing about African trees, it could be a completely different category of trees.

[2] It had been a long time since I had given up on sleeping bags and backpacks, which were far too bulky and useless in hot countries.

7 years on the road

In the morning, I wake up in a good mood, as usual, and I see the lady of the house pounding millet. She gives me a little sign to mean hello. I do the same and start getting ready to hit the road again. I shake out my blanket, roll it up, and tie it with my turban so I can carry it on my shoulder. And I take my hat that was lying on the ground. And there, surprise: a snake was coiled inside. It wakes up and starts to crawls slowly toward the forest. The lady who was pounding millet seems afraid and makes me understand with gestures that I must kill the poor snake. She insists heavily, completely panicked. So I take a stick and kill this poor snake that was not yet fully awake.
The lady is happy, but not me. The snake had made itself warm under my black hat and hadn't noticed that day had broken. The rules of hospitality among humans leave something to be desired...

In the middle of the Sahel, a bush taxi picks me up. It's a pickup truck with a dozen passengers crammed into the back. After a few hours, a breakdown occurs. Usually, it's the tires, smooth as baby skin, that burst. No, this time it's a shock absorber that breaks.
There's no way to continue. The driver and his greaser don't panic, however: a palm branch does the trick. They tie it up with some completely flat inner tubes, and we finally arrive in Ouagadougou, where I meet a French friend, also a backpacker and junkie.

He injects himself I don't know what, in the restrooms of the youth center where we're staying. To thank the director, we decide to put on a clown show for him and his employees. It's crap, absolutely crap. We're the only ones who die laughing. It must be said that we smoke like chimneys before going on stage. But no one says anything to us. They probably thought the same of us.

The adventure is cut short, and a particularly aggressive case of malaria sends me to the hospital. This is the opportunity to taste my first quinine injection. I will have many more. My fever quickly falls, and one evening I escape to go party with my African friends. I am kicked out the next day by the white nun who is looking after me. And there, I decide to return to Niger.

For some reason, I'm crossing the Niger River in a dugout canoe. I'm not at all reassured, especially since a herd of hippos isn't far away. The Africans explain to me that they're "mean." In fact, hippos are at home in the warm waters of the

7 years on the road

Niger River, and they're defending their territory. If you keep your distance, there's no problem.

One morning in Niamey, I was awakened by Nigerien police officers who, following a tip-off, came to arrest me for possession of cannabis. They quickly sent me to see their boss. He was French, a former boss of the "Evêché[1]" in Marseille.

I was sent to prison, but I only stayed there for a few minutes. I had barely arrived when I was told I was being released and deported[2]. It was the French consul who intervened with my parents, without asking me anything. I learned this when I arrived in Brittany. For him, it was inconceivable that a white person would be in prison in Niger. It wouldn't have bothered me. After Les Baumettes, the prison in Marseille, the little I saw of the prison seemed very cool. Living conditions were quite basic but in a good mood.
I'm flying in a 707. It's my first time on an airplane. Another experience.

---

[1] The central police station.
[2] All this without trial, of course.

The serious stuff begins

I'm returning to Brittany. I'm stopping off in Rennes. In a bistro, I meet a group of young people with varying degrees of hair. At that time, backpackers like me were rare and a source of inspiration. After a while, Glenmor, the Breton bard who reawakened Brittany in the 1960s, enters, surrounded by a group of young people. I didn't yet know that I would meet him later.

Glenmor (Millig for friends)

7 years on the road

I return to Rennes after visiting my parents in St-Brieuc to thank them and at the same time reproach them, gently though they were, for having repatriated me. They should have let me go to prison; it was part of the life I had chosen. I accepted it.

I meet up with the gang of rogues I knew in the café where Glenmor had arrived. We hang around Place Sainte-Anne for a bit. I stay with a few others at a couple's house. There isn't a single bit of hashish for sale at that time[1], so we console ourselves with products available over the counter in pharmacies.

One day, one of their friends "lent" us her parents' apartment, while they were away. We settled in with a few pharmaceutical products to spend the night. It was a dull evening until the friend's father stormed into his house and kicked us all out. A stupid little incident that would have repercussions later on.

This story displeased me, and I decided to hit the road again. A rumor was circulating in the small, marginalized Rennes scene: the Rolling Stones were going to play a concert in Marrakech. We all promised to meet up there. And so, I decided to go.

I'm crossing France again, but with no intention of stopping. I'm heading straight for Marseille.

Problem: I don't have enough money to take the boat, and I have no desire to go through Franco's Spain. So, I'm going to the Mérieux Institute to sell my blood.

Off to Algeria! I'm not hanging around here either. I'm heading straight for Morocco.

I arrived first. Djemaa El Fna Square is crowded. Since arriving in Morocco, I've been in awe almost constantly. Marrakech doesn't yet have a Club Med, and tourists are rare in January 1970.

After asking around, I realized that the rumor was just that. The Stones did have a villa in Marrakech, but that was it. One day, I saw Mick Jagger crossing the Djemaa El Fna square, deep in conversation with another guy I didn't know.

Well, I'm in Morocco, with or without the guys from Rennes, it's the same. My father told me a lot about it. He spent eight years there before and during the war.

---

[1] In 2024, drug gangs are killing each other. Prohibition is reminiscent of the alcohol prohibition of Al Capone's time.

7 years on the road

Moroccans smoke kif—cannabis cut with fresh black tobacco—almost openly. Patrolling cops always look the other way when they spot a sibsi—a kif pipe. I think this country is great. Obviously, I don't know Hassan II's domestic politics...
In the medinas, all women are veiled, except the Berbers who wear henna makeup.

Every time I have the opportunity to pass through Fez, I stop at the exit where a hermit has built a hut with everything he can find: branches, various scraps of household appliances, plastic sheeting... We call him Boulehaya – I think it means "the bearded one[1]".

In the evening, his friends meet at his place and smoke kif while sharing a bottle of wine. That's half a small glass each. It's enough to boost the kif. He has several small pouches that he wedges between the branches of his cabin. They sing while clapping their hands. With them, I am happy.

But one day, on my way back from Marrakech, there was no more cabin. I was deeply disappointed and was about to leave the city when I met Boulehaya. And then, infinite sadness. The hermit was drunk and reeked of methylated spirits; he didn't recognize me and seemed half-mad.

---

[1]But I wouldn't swear to it.

This methylated spirits is a real mess. In Morocco, you can find wine—el shrab—but it's forbidden for Moroccans. So there are red wine dealers, but they're rare, because it's very heavily repressed. So Moroccans who want a drink turn to methylated spirits, which quickly fries their brains. I feel so sorry for Boulehaya. From a hermit, he's become a bum.

Occasionally, I'll buy a liter of red wine from the shops that sell it to tourists, for the Moroccans waiting for me outside. If it can save them from having to drink methylated spirits...

I meet "freaks" everywhere. It's an American term that encompasses anything hairy, smoking, and moving. It's much less reductive than hippy, beatnik, or backpacker. Americans almost all have the same background: they worked for a year before leaving for London. From there, they go to Germany, where they buy a Volkswagen minibus and go down to Morocco. Many of them are draft dodgers. They're fleeing the Vietnam War. They like everyone except the French and Moroccans, who are considered thieves.

A few people gather in the evening around a large table on the terrace of a café in Djemaa el Fna Square. I sit down, but one of them immediately signals me not to continue:
— No French here.
To which I reply:
— I am not French, I am Breton.
They chat a little among themselves and invite me to sit down. I take out my sibsi and offer each of them a pipe.

I understand their reaction. A gang of junkies, mostly from Nice, specializes in stealing Traveller's Checks and passports. I'm still a bit stunned. They seem to know the difference between a Breton and a Frenchman, even though they have no idea about European geography. I couldn't understand what they were saying. Later, I learned that among them was an Englishman, who had explained to them that we were like the Welsh to the English, and therefore like Native Americans to the Americans.

Life in Marrakech at the very beginning of spring is very pleasant. No rain and the heat is very bearable. I meet lots of people. We smoke kif and hashish. For the latter, I discover the chillum. An Indian clay pipe with no bend. You inhale directly into the hand holding it; the other serves as a support and ensures a seal. The "smack" is immediate and significantly stronger than a four- or six-skin joint.

Djemaa el Fana Square in the evening, Marrakech

Conversations no longer revolve around Istanbul, but rather around India, which at that time was called "The Indies." I meet people who are going there, others who are returning. These people are visibly moved. They have something in their eyes that the others don't. It intrigues me, and I would like to know more.

And then there's a lot of talk about Acid. Lysergic acid diethylamide derived from rye ergot. The famous LSD 25 stolen from the US army by Timothy Leary, whom I would meet a few months later in Algiers.

I want to try it. I talk to a friend who knows a lot about it. He advises me not to try it in Marrakech because of the crowds and suggests I go to Essaouira, which is on the ocean. He also tells me that it's a journey within oneself and that it's necessary to have a guide. It's especially important not to do it alone the first time.

After a few days, I went to Essaouira. The Portuguese influence on the scenery was clearly felt. In front of the ramparts, a beautiful beach was swept by a constant wind that ruined everything.

Essaouira one of the city gates

I met a Frenchman. He tells me there's a small village a few kilometers away at the end of the beach. There are lots of freaks living there. The Moroccans organize themselves to rent out as many houses as possible.

I decide to go there. The town is called Diabet. It is connected to Essaouira beach by an impassable bridge. All that remains is a stone border. The rest has collapsed. If we don't choose this route, we'll have to take a long detour.

It is a small village with no running water, no electricity, and no motor vehicles other than the Volkswagen vans of American hippies.

In Diabet, there's only one grocery store run by a smart old man who rips us off as much as he can. His shop is open every day. He sleeps in it at night.

He mainly sells batteries for those who have audio cassettes. It's time for Neil Young; Crosby, Still and Nash; Jefferson Airplane; Jimmy Hendrix, Janis Joplin; Cat Stevens; Grateful Dead and especially Pink Floyd.
For some time now I have been wearing only a blue gandoura and sandals. I have a blanket, a sweater and jeans rolled up in it, my chillum which I wear as a neck lace and my passport in the pocket of the gandoura, that's all.

What remains of the bridge a few years later.

I have a few friends, and I live with a small group in a one-room house. We spend our time smoking and talking about travel, the adventures and misadventures we encountered in Turkey or Iran. But what I like most is when we host someone who has just returned from India.

7 years on the road

One day, an American woman introduced me to the I Ching. She practices the three-coin method. I toss the coins six times in a row, without question. I get the first hexagram: the Creator. She looks at me strangely and asks me to start again. Which I do. I land on the Creator. She wants me to start again, and I get the same thing again. She ends up telling me that she'd never had a case like mine. So, she offers me a fix—an intravenous injection—of amphetamines. I'd never taken any, and she pushes half the box into my bloodstream and swallows the other fifteen pills the same way.

I'm discovering that there are two ways to manage the effect. Either you put your physical appearance first and find yourself at three in the morning running, in falsely good shape, along the beach in Essaouira, or you internalize everything. This is the option I choose. I find a corner in the house, sit cross-legged with my back straight against a wall. And for seven to eight hours my brain works at full capacity, without the slightest movement on my part. The support for reflection I choose is the need to find what I'm looking for, that is, the direction and the goal to achieve.

I'm served. The direction is East, and the goal is total poverty. Well, the amphetamines weren't necessary for the goal: I'm completely broke, and I like it enormously, even if it poses technical problems, like eating, for example. That's the price of freedom. The desire to go to India was already present before the fix. But it has become almost vital because it is the only place in the world where total poverty is venerated, when it is voluntary, of course. These hours spent cooking my brain, so intense was the exaltation, completely confirm for me that I must go to India to live there.

The descent is extremely painful. Fortunately, because I already know that you become addicted very quickly. And that this is serious. I've seen enough junkies to be convinced of this.

Armed with this observation, I began to read everything I could find, in French and English – which was a bit difficult for me, concerning India. The Bhagavad Gita, the aphorisms of Sri Aurobindo, the Tibetan Book of the Dead, the Kena-Upanishad, etc.

7 years on the road

One day, while I was preparing a tagine in the house where I lived, two people arrived, causing a mini-inner earthquake. A brother and a sister. He had something in his eyes that announced he had seen what could not be seen. What could not be explained. She was dressed in a red sari and exuded holiness. They were welcomed, of course. They accepted my invitation to eat. They told us about their experiences in India. He, Jean-Jacques, only spent three months in Goa, Banares, Manali, and Kathmandu. He had frequented a few Shaivite Sâdhus. He explained to me that these Sâdhus were renunciants. They had experienced the ultimate: the Atman-Brahman fusion, that is, the union of the individual soul and the universal soul. They have become immortal—not physically, of course. They own nothing. This is the height of wealth.

He took an "Acid" in Banares—Varanasī in Hindi or Sanskrit—with one of them. According to the latter, they attained Samadhi: the state of consciousness obtained by opening the chakra located at the top of the skull. A yogi will devote his entire life to it, perhaps, to achieve it. With Acid, it is immediate. This claim is rejected by many gurus and doctors. But the reverse is also the case. We will discuss this later.

When he talks about Shiva, whom he calls Shankar—one of his 108 names—he completely captivates me. His sister, Yolande, became a disciple of a rather unusual guru. He calls himself "Father" and has been living in California for several months. He's what I call, with a bit of irony, a "successful" guru. I don't believe for a moment in the sanctity of English-speaking gurus and swamis, who specialize in Westerners in search of themselves. Preferably an American Westerner, and if possible, not too poor.

Jean-Jacques offers to guide me on my first trip. I enthusiastically accept. We decide to do it outside under the stars. We smoke a few chillums while waiting for the LSD to kick in. And after a while, my level of consciousness expands, I feel overwhelmed by a gigantic happiness that makes me merge with the Universe. Pure ecstasy!

The inexplicable is difficult to explain, so the ineffable... But I will try. There are necessarily two "me's". One, with a body, and another "me", not very different, which is perfectly integrated into the universe and observes what is happening. The ego is completely silent, even absent. I am perfectly aware of the situation. It is indeed I who am in communion with what I call "the Great Whole", but I take no glory from it, and I do not try to bring anything back to me, that is to say to my ego. I am content to live fully in the present moment and then, something becomes obvious: **I have understood everything!!!** : that is all that matters. Everything else exists[1], or not, but it has no importance, it is the illusion: Maya. Only that moment counts. Later I would learn that the Indians call it Sat-Cit-Ananda: Being-Consciousness-Bliss.

Contrary to what is often said, we don't hear anything special, we don't see anything special. If we can say we have "seen God" or the "Light," it is an image. We don't see angels blowing trumpets, we have no contact with beings of light... None of that. No special effects. It is only the blossoming of consciousness in to tal bliss.

The descent is gentle after twelve hours, and there I realize that I have just been born again. I am therefore a Dvija – a twice-born. This trip has been a second birth. It's clear, it's sharp and indisputable. I no longer see anything the same way. I can almost read an individual's soul after a simple glance at their face. It's another Hervé who has just been born. Not very different from the other one, but radically different nonetheless.

Nothing matters. Everything exists, but it doesn't matter. Good and evil don't matter, nothing does, in fact. Only the fusion with the "Greater Whole" matters. The concept of Maya is similar to that of the quantum universe, derived from the physics of the same name.

I can't talk about God. Does he exist? If so, which one? I don't know. I'm an atheist; if I had been a believer, I probably would have had a different interpretation. It doesn't matter. No vision of Shiva or Jesus; we are beyond the conception of God. There will be some later, once we come back down to earth.

I discuss this with Jean-Jacques and others. For them, there is a god who is the union of all that exists, whom they call Shiva[2] or Shankar; he is present, every-

---

[1] Universe, galaxies, sense of duty, human society, illness, love, hate, life, death, in short everything.

[2] Shiva, like all gods and goddesses, are "manifestations" of Brahman, just like me, you, and the chair I am sitting in.

where and in everything. I am Shiva, you too, and the Universe too (matter, emotions, feelings, thoughts included).

In fact, he's present in all elementary particles, quarks, photons, protons, and antiprotons… That's what my brain deduces to try to find a relatively rational explanation. Shiva is the king of quantum physics. He is Consciousness. he's in everything and is just waiting for energy—Shakti—to merge. Shakti is in each of us. It's up to us to set it in motion and introduce it to Shiva. Acid is one way. There are hundreds of others.

If it helps me understand, I'm not at all sure that any physicist would follow me. Completely transformed by this experience, I decided to go to India and live there as a Sâdhu until my death.

7 years on the road

7 years on the road

A short tour of the Maghreb

What was feared has just happened: plainclothes cops. Nothing serious, but a passport and visa check. One of them tells me it's time to leave; I entered Morocco more than six months ago on a three-month visa.

I accept without hesitation. It's just that things have to happen this way. Yet I don't feel ready enough to go to India alone. I'm going to take a trip to Tunisia and come back with a new visa.

I set off with Jean-Jacques, hitchhiking towards Algiers. He's heading back to Marseille, where he lives. We pass through Casablanca, which wasn't my usual route. As we cross the medina of Casablanca, I hear someone calling my name. We look up and see one of the guys who was at Diabet, at the edge of a terrace, beckoning us up. Which we do.

There are about ten freaks around a low table busy testing all sorts of different hashish. It ranges from dark green to black to white—the one that's been buried for a year. The friend who called me explains that two Americans want to buy a kilo. The seller, a Moroccan in his thirties, signals us to go ahead and test everything we want. So, we go! The chillums, joints, and water pipes come into play, and we test everything. After a while, everyone is stoned, and we have the greatest difficulty deciding which hash is the best. Finally, the American leading the transaction chooses one.

The Moroccan goes to get the kilo and comes back very quickly with a bag. He looks everywhere, trying to spot any curious onlookers, and exchanges money for hash under the coffee table. The American doesn't check what the Moroccan is handing him. Once the transaction is complete, the Moroccan greets everyone and leaves. The American decides to inaugurate his kilo and discreetly takes out a plate to make a chillum. And then, disaster strikes, he realizes he's just bought a kilo of henna! He tries to find the Moroccan, but obviously the other one hasn't waited for him...

7 years on the road

We set off again towards Oujda. On the other side of the border, we meet an American who offers to put us up for the night in a large shared room rented from a hotel. There are at least twenty people, sitting on mats, leaning against the walls. We have plenty of marijuana and hashish; it must be said that at that time, people crossed the border with whatever they wanted in their pockets, quite naturally. Sibsis, chillums, and joints are passed around. Three candles, on copper trays, light the room. I can make out the one playing the darbuka through the smoke.

Someone knocks at the door, causing a violent silence that makes everyone land. Algeria isn't Morocco. It's very repressive when it comes to cannabis. It's the hotel owner. He asks who Monsieur Le Bévillon is. He has my passport in his hand. I get up, completely stoned. I'm convinced they'll notice. The two plainclothes cops waiting for me at the bottom of the stairs scrutinize me. I smile while panicking inwardly. They ask me if I plan to stay in Algeria. I tell them I'm going to Tunisia. Throughout this interview, which I find extremely long, they scrutinize me straight in the eyes. Then, the older of the two gives me back my passport and wishes me goodnight. Phew!

It's a harsh reality check. Shiva may be everywhere and in everything, but that doesn't mean life doesn't go on, even if it doesn't matter. It's up to each of us to come to terms with it, to rise above this petty, ridiculous life. We just have to figure out how to do it.

Arriving in Algiers, I looked for a place in the center to exhibit my drawings made with the gang of rascals from Rennes. They are awful. They are more or less geometric patterns, each crossed out with dozens of lines made in black pen. They are A4 format. I hold them to the ground with stones. Jean-Jacques writes the traditional: "Help us continue our journey."

The coins fall immediately. Not big ones, but lots of small ones. That helps. After an hour, we have enough for breakfast. We go to a dairy at the entrance to the Casbah. They have buttermilk[1], which they call elben (and leben in Morocco). We have enough to buy ourselves some warm baguettes. The dairyman sells us butter. I have to ask him for salt, because a Breton can't eat unsalted butter without denying his soul. That's how it is.

---

[1] Milk after being churned.

In the evening, a small group of students invites us to their home. When we arrive, there are already about ten African Americans, Black Panther political refugees, and two gorgeous Algerians accompanied by two very beautiful French women. Two sisters.

The chillums and bottles of red wine are circulating. Jean-Jacques and I aren't drinking, but the sisters are getting increasingly heated. After trying their luck with us in vain, they turn to the Americans, who jump at the chance. And then, things get downright heated...

The Casbah of Algiers

In the evening, a guy in his forties with a girl old enough to be his daughter comes and sits down a little to one side. It's Timothy Leary, who's hiding in Algeria with all the American cops on his tail.

Timothy Leary

7 years on the road

I hesitate to tell him that thanks to him, I've just had a fantastic experience. But I know I'm far from the only one, so I leave him alone. Plus, he's obviously more interested in his girlfriend than anything else.

The next day we're staying with another student. We go because the Black Panthers are good, but we quickly get tired of the drunken partying, and then watching them screw French women in the middle of the room is a bit awkward. The two Algerians remain chaste. Their father makes them take a virginity certificate every month. So they wait until they're adults.

A few days later, Jean-Jacques uses his return ticket to reach Marseille. I'm going to Tunis. Hitchhiking in Algeria, and even throughout the Maghreb, is a pleasure. I stick out my thumb and two cars stop. The people are always very open, friendly, and warm. As usual, I'm invited everywhere except one evening when I arrive in a town I don't know, and there I go to eat at the Red Crescent. It's the Muslim version of the Red Cross. The Muslim Brotherhood finances it. Volunteers wearing red American caps run the shop. No one asks me for anything. It's good and the atmosphere is nice.

Arriving in Tunis, I head out to see the medina. Not far from the entrance, there are steps in front of a more or less official building, on which all sorts of hairy individuals, more Western than North African, are waiting. I stay with them for a while.

Tunis Medina

7 years on the road

I also meet some Tunisian students. We become friends, and during an impromptu party, I'm treated to a special belly dance. It's very erotic when it's special, especially when it's not in traditional costume. But it won't go any further. I'm not in the mood for it.

On the steps of a building on Avenue Bourguiba, without really noticing it, I find myself chatting with a guy with a Parisian accent and long hair. His name is Daniel[1]. He is part of a group of young people from the Guy-Moquet Square in Paris, transported by their priest to North Africa to take their minds off things.

He has two acids on him and would like to try it. He's never been on a trip before, and I suggest we spend the night outside the city under the stars. He agrees and goes to ask the priest for his "blessing" for the night. He looks at me askance but finally agrees. Daniel takes his sleeping bag and we go looking for a quiet spot. We finally find it by the sea. Since it's his first trip, I act as his guide. We both spend the night in communion with the sky, the earth, the sea, and everything that exists. This "trip" confirms the first ones, as it does practically all those I will take until my return from Black Africa—we'll talk about it again. It's really what I felt the first time. There are two "me's," the one who merges in full communion with the universe and the other who admires this phenomenon. We don't say a word. What would we talk about? We live intensely in the present moment. We are Shiva, Acid has triggered Shakti. We bathe in Unity.

In the early morning, we come down from our trip. Daniel returns to his priest, and I "bouine"—I laze around, as they say in Gallo, the language of Upper Brittany. I wait on the steps. The acid was truly top-notch. The weather is nice, the atmosphere is friendly on Avenue Bourguiba. Why move, why run?

But, I set off again towards the post office, I have a letter from my parents waiting for me there. At the time we didn't call each other. I had agreed with my mother, who was beside herself with anxiety, to send her a letter, even without a stamp or anything in it, to give a sign of life. We stayed in touch via the general delivery service. No problem, I'll go. The employee gives me my letter and asks me for 40 millimes – because in Tunisia, at that time, at least, they were starting to count in millimes of Dinars. I don't have a penny, as usual, and I turn around to see if I can ask someone for them and then, I have practically the only real hallu

---

[1]That's not his real first name.

cination of my entire life: I find myself in the middle of a cartoon. All the users and postal workers have transformed into caricatures of themselves. Big noses, big ears, all the distinctive features are exaggerated. I burst out laughing and everything goes back to normal. The first guy I ask for 40 millimes gives it to me without any problem.

Forty years later, after reading all sorts of accounts of NDE-like experiences, I think that if my mind had been tortured, I might have freaked out when I found myself in this other dimension, but a burst of laughter was enough. My ego was truly put aside.

Daniel decides to continue with me to Morocco and says goodbye to his priest, who doesn't appreciate it at all. We pass through Rabat, which wasn't the route I usually took. There, in the evening, we go begging on the main street of Rabat. We come across two Moroccans who tell us they don't have any money but know a place where we can sleep peacefully.

Okay, we're following. We're feeling good, we'll eat tomorrow. And then we're starting to think we're going a bit far. We're leaving the city; it's almost dark. Finally, we land in a cemetery, the one in Salé, a suburb of Rabat.

Rabat, city center

There, they find two rotten mats, lay them on the floor, and sit on them. OK, we take out the sibsie and start smoking. And then the two guys get enterprising. Ouch, there's been a mistake! We tell them, they take it badly and get the idea to rob us, to compensate. There, no problem, I tell them to search and keep all the money they find.

Salé Cemetery

Obviously, they find nothing. And in a rage, they manage to rip off Daniel's pants and leave immediately. Daniel is in his underwear. I give him my gandoura. Since he's smaller than me, he steps on it. But, it's better than nothing. We go to see the cops in Rabat who tell us there's nothing they can do, but we end up finding a pair of jeans roughly his size. Daniel is disgusted, he goes back to Paris.

7 years on the road

7 years on the road

Heading India

Here I am back in Diabet, where life goes on without me. I meet up with friends and make new ones, including Christian, his head shaved with just a ponytail, like a "Hare-Krisna." He freaked out in Marrakech when he ran into the gang of Nice residents who specialize in stealing passports and travelers' checks, without disdaining cash.

They gave him Acid as if he were an old friend, they dropped him off in Djemaa el-Fna square among snake charmers, Gnawa Berbers, kids dancing barefoot on broken bottles, etc. They rushed to search his bag to steal everything. He noticed the theft while he was going down. He was a bit weirded out. It's this group of junkies who rot everything in their path. This is the first time I've seen collateral damage from Acid. I'll see more. It makes me think about the positions taken by some and others through the press. Yes, it's definitely a dangerous product if taken haphazardly. But taken in the same conditions as me, it's extremely positive.

Besides, I'm taking others, alone now, but with the necessary conditions: at night under the stars, away from the noise and away from the crowd, as usual. I take one every other day for a while.

That night, I walk around Diabet, in a gandoura, my blanket over my shoulders. And suddenly, I realize that I am no longer in my body but right next to it. My mind or my second "self" is like a walking companion. I am next to "me" while being in "me." It is impossible to explain clearly, especially to someone who knows neither LSD nor the search for Shiva-Shakti fusion.

And yet, we're in it. For me, it's not even debatable. It's just the way it is. I don't have any hallucinations, apart from a few original perceptions of material reality. The colors are more vivid, everything is beautiful. I fully enjoy the present moment, merging with the "Great Whole" in an immense happiness that completely overwhelms me.

7 years on the road

And then life goes on in Diabet. I often prepare vegetable tagines. It makes a dish for about ten people. So we take bread to eat it, like the Moroccans. All this between two chillums. We often go to Essaouira via the beach.

One of the guys from Rennes arrived one day and moved in with us in Diabet. Later, I learned that the whole gang had gotten into trouble with the cops over drug use at the party I was attending at a friend's house. The father had filed a complaint for drug use, even though there weren't any. When the investigation began, I was already in Morocco and I didn't know anything about it. The whole gang accused me. Of course, I wasn't there. At the trial, I received a six-month suspended sentence in absentia for "advocating drugs." The cops waited for me until I returned from Africa to notify me of my sentence and ask me if I wanted to appeal or not.

Life in Diabet depends on the weather. In winter, there aren't many people. Only a few houses are rented. I make a friend: Larbi, one of the local guys who rents out his house. As soon as spring arrives, the American hippies arrive too. We spend our time smoking and taking acid. We also make opium tea: it's poppy husks that we buy for next to nothing at the market. We have to boil them. It's disgusting to drink, but it has a slight effect.

One evening, we went to some American friends' house in another village. A Moroccan, who earned his keep preaching in the local markets, was in charge of making a hashish cake. The chillums were playing almost to the rhythm of the darboukas. A French friend gave me a fix of amphetamines. It went up right away. Someone must have a large stash of hash, because the chillums were constantly being played.

The cake is ready. The cakes, more precisely. The Moroccan saw that several would be needed. I take a large slice. He's strong! After a few minutes, I'm off again, like the other time with the American woman at the I Ching. Nothing happens outside, everything unfolds in my head. But I go out because I've just decided to learn more. I want to intellectualize the fusion I experienced during my trips. I stay in the courtyard of the small adobe house, all alone in the night. I look at the sky, standing under the rhythms of the darboukas. And there, internally, I question the sky: " 1Do you exist God? If so, give me a sign." I immediately receive an answer. The universe contracts for a fraction of a second. I take it right to

7 years on the road

the heart. It was only meant for me, no one could have noticed. It is a clear, clean and precise yes.

I'm a bit stunned into the night, then I go back into the house. I sit down in the corner where I was and suddenly I start to cry for no apparent reason. In fact I re ceive a very long message and I immediately write down what is sent to me, in a small notebook that I will destroy later, stupidly, in black Africa. I am completely incapable of remembering the exact content now. And it goes on and on! The pages fill up...

I stayed in Diabet for a few days, more silent than usual. I had an answer, it's un deniable. A Cartesian would tell me that these were only the effects of a drug. In deed, there were even two: the hashish cake and the amphetamines, not to mention the chillums. But these drugs allowed this questioning and the answer, no doubt, as well. But it was only intended for me. For no one else. And the answer comes from me, from my unconscious, from what I already know, since God is not someone else. Each experience is individual, necessarily. It depends on each person and is not entirely transferable to others. It is necessarily a solitary quest. Not necessarily alone in the desert, but also in normal life. This dual experience left a strong impression on me. I imagine that this is the kind of thing that the monotheistic prophets experienced, without amphetamines[1], of course. But, ultimately, since I have no intention of founding a religion, it doesn't matter.

But I'm not entirely satisfied. It's time I headed to India, I know I'll find the answer there.

In Oujda, I take a bus to Algeria, but it can't start because a police car cuts it off with a loud screech of tires, American-style. The cops come straight towards me and take me away. In France it was routine, in Morocco it's more surprising. My papers are checked and I'm put in jail. I have hashish on me, but they don't search me. In fact, I'm deported; my visa is still several months overdue. After a fairly short while, they send me to the border.

There, the customs officer or chief cop decides to make me wait. He's probably hoping I'll beg him to let me pass, but I have a book and I start reading quietly, es

---

[1] But probably ephedra.

pecially since I'm still high from the morning joint. A fascinating book, it's the cop who cracks first and gets me across the border.

Oujda 1900

The route I propose to follow is quite simple: the Algerian, Tunisian, Libyan, Egyptian coasts and then I will see if I can go through Jordan or Israel and reach Iran, Afghanistan, Pakistan and India.

In Algiers, I meet Michel, a tall, hairy man from Vendée. He's managed to get hold of some hashish. He stops in front of my scribble exhibition. He's amused to see Algerians giving change. I have to refuse a coin given to me by a supposedly blind beggar, sitting further away. He persists, and finally I accept his cents. In two hours, we have enough money not only to buy more hashish, but also to treat ourselves to a monstrous breakfast at my usual dairy, even though it's long past noon.

He's going to India too. He doesn't have a cent but doesn't hesitate to beg, unlike me who doesn't like it at all. We do one last exhibition the next day. We earn a tiny bit more money, and we hitchhike east.

We reached the Libyan border without difficulty. We barely saw Tunisia outside the brothel district of Sfax, where the guy who picked us up absolutely insisted on taking a break. We waited outside the brothel. Not because of excessive prudishness, but it wasn't our thing at the time. And, as far as I'm concerned, I need a minimum of affection.

Algiers, the big post office.

Libyan customs officers search all bags and suitcases looking for pornographic photos, alcohol, or any other prohibited goods that they are likely to seize. For Michel and me, it's done quickly. However, we don't have Libyan visas, and they refuse to let us in. Usually, we would get a three-month tourist visa at the border, but not here.

A U-turn towards Tunis, heading for the Libyan embassy. There's one image I'll keep in mind: the highway, which begins behind the Libyan border post, lit by sodium streetlights diffusing an orange glow. The contrast is striking. Although Tunisia isn't exactly a very poor country, Libya, or at least what we saw of it, feels almost like Europe.
We grumble, but it's no use, we need that damn visa. Before turning around, we watch with amusement, on the Tunisian side, as the Libyans feast in an open-air

restaurant with copious amounts of red wine, aperitifs, and whiskey. A Tunisian explains to us that Libyans who can afford it come all the way to the border to have fun because alcohol is severely repressed back home.

Well, here we are, heading back to Tunis. It's a little frustrating, but there's no get ting around it. A quick trip, just long enough to get that visa. We dine in a café with a bottle of Koudia, a big red that's very popular. We order a bottle and the owner keeps bringing us hearty appetizers. It goes down so well that we order a second one. Then we head, slightly staggering, towards Avenue Mohamed V where soft grass grows between the palm trees on either side. It's an excellent mattress and there's almost no traffic. We sleep soundly.

As usual in North Africa, hitchhiking is easy. The first car that passes on this highway stops. It's going to Tripoli, which is good, so are we. We immediately sense that the country is rich. Chatting with the guy who picked us up, we discover that there are about three million Libyans, that they have enormous underground wealth. They have European aid workers. Tunisian workers do the toughest jobs, but are apparently quite well paid. The driver is proud to have Gaddafi as his leader. It must be said that we only see him on posters, in the streets. He is relatively young and handsome. He has a special guard of six sexy young women armed to the teeth, combat sports champions and snipers. He lives only in his tent, set up behind the presidential palace.

But there's one slight problem: alcohol is strictly forbidden. Five years in prison for public drunkenness, and twenty years for manufacturing alcohol. Libyans are thirsty. "We live like horses," an old man told me. "We work, we eat, and we sleep, but that's all."

Tripoli is a very pleasant city. A bit like Algiers. It must be significantly warmer inland. Michel and I stay on the seafront. It's a beautiful city, clean and wealthy, but it doesn't appeal to us. We don't know why. So we pack up our gear and head east, towards Benghazi, the country's second largest city.

It's better there. Still the appearance of a calm city, where life is good. There is significantly less population than in Tripoli. We notice that there are almost no women in the streets. We know about Islam and how they are treated. But here, it's different. They seem to be completely excluded from the society..

Muammar Gaddafi, young and handsome. It won't last.

Yet, from time to time, we see a few veiled ones. And even, much more rarely, others dressed in Western clothes.

We meet a Frenchman, a technical development worker. He explains what he does, but we don't really listen. He invites us to follow him to his home. And there, it's almost like a beer lover's cave. He has dozens of racks of empty bottles on one side and full ones on the other. He opens his fridge and offers us one. We gladly accept. It's a beer fridge. He has another one for everyday use.

Benghazi

It's strong and not really good. But, we're not going to be picky. He then takes us to the home of one of his English colleagues. He's also a clandestine brewer. He's much nicer than the Frenchman who had a slightly embarrassing redneck side. He invites us to his home for as long as we like. We've long since lost track of time, but, well, no problem. We settle into a room with a big rug, which is a change from the rocks we're used to.

He gives us the beer recipe: A fifty-liter trash can, fill it with water and add a can of Biomalt. You can buy it at the pharmacy. Next, you need the juice of thirty limes, three kilos of sugar, and a tablespoon of yeast. Mix and let it sit until a thin crust appears. Then, you have to bottle the beer. Finally, he shows us a capper. It's the opposite of a bottle opener. It pushes the cap in. You have to tap it with a shoe. Once these operations are completed, he leaves the bottles in the racks and a few weeks later, he stores them in his fridge.

7 years on the road

One day, while we were strolling in a square by the sea, about ten students came to see us. Among them were Palestinians wearing keffiyehs. It was the first time I'd seen them. They were friendly and dressed in Western clothes. They asked us where we came from, where we were going, etc. They were curious. We told them we were going to Egypt, and they informed us that the road was cut off due to disagreements between Colonel Gaddafi and Anwar Sadat, the Egyptian president. When we told them how we earned our keep with my great drawings, they laughed heartily and explained to us how we should do it. Two of them went off for a few minutes and wrote two pages in their notebooks in Arabic. They gave us one each. They told us how to proceed. We have to choose a shopping street in the souk, enter without a word, simply say: "Salam Aleïcum" hand the paper to the shopkeeper and he will give us money. We remain a little incredulous. They explain to us that they have written several verses of the Koran explaining that the one who travels must be helped by the sedentary; that it is a duty for believers; that it is essential to help foreigners. In short, with that we should be able to get by.

After thanking our British host, we go to the souk to test our "Koranic visa." We divide up the street. Michel does the jewelers and I do the drapers. I enter my first shop where the owner is calmly reading a newspaper. I say "Salam Aleicum" and hand him the paper. He reads it, takes a note from his cash register, puts it in the folded notebook sheet, and hands it to me. I say "shoukran"—thank you—and I leave. I join Michel. We can hardly believe it. It worked perfectly. We decide to walk the whole street and then we'll see. When we've finished the street, we have enough money for two 4plane tickets from Benghazi to Cairo, enough to each buy a small Arab vest, and we have a dollar left.

A few hours later we land in Cairo.

7 years on the road

From Egypt to Sudan

Cairo! This is a change. Compared to prosperous and calm Libya, Egypt seems a bit like an anthill of excited people. Everyone is shouting and jostling in every corner of the airport.

A huge queue forms. This is where we have to declare our money, just like in Algeria. I walk over to a fat, uniformed cop, rifle slung over his shoulder, who smiles beatifically as he watches the queue.
I explain to him that we only have a dollar, and that it would be ridiculous to stand in that line. He sympathizes but thinks it's a bit tight to enter his country. I explain that we have money in the bank and at the post office. He doesn't believe a word of it, but it's enough for him and he lets us through.

All the taxis want to drive us, but when we explain that we only have a dollar, they don't insist.

Cairo 1967

7 years on the road

For people who like overcrowded and hysterical cities, Cairo is a great place to be. We are completely stunned to see the trams, or trolleys, overcrowded. There are more people hanging on the outside than crammed inside. And, to our great surprise, there are ticket collectors. They manage to squeeze between the passengers. They are all very thin, after all; it must be an impossible job for fat people.

Tram. Cairo, 1935. Not much had changed.

The city is under siege. In front of every public building, there's a sign that says "No photos." And to make it clear that things are serious, a machine gun pokes its nose out from between the sandbags.

Men's fashion is all about battle dress. We assume Egypt is at war with Israel. But that's just an assumption; we haven't cared about current events for a long time. Vendors selling cigarettes and other odds and ends also stock military braids that can be sewn on yourself or attached with a safety pin, which is sold with them. There are a lot of "ranking officers" on the streets.

The shopkeepers try to get us into their stores. It's not yet noon, but we sense we're going to have trouble finding a place to sleep. We talk to lots of people, but we sense that traditional Muslim hospitality won't work.

Evening arrives and we still haven't found anything. This has never happened to me in Africa! We're exhausted and fed up. An idea comes to me: we head straight to the police station, which we find quite easily. I ask the head cop to lend us a cell for the night. He politely refuses. For once, I'm the one asking to be put in a cell, and they refuse!

The head cop offers to let us sleep in a mosque. I like it. Michel does too. We've never seen one from the inside. The cop takes us to the most beautiful one we've ever seen.
He chats for a few moments with an old man who is counting his beads. He agrees and signals us to wait. Which we do.

Later we learn that this is the El Azhar Mosque, the headquarters of the Muslim Brotherhood.

El Azhar Mosque, at the time there were no cars in front of it, nor a gate.

At that time, there were no bloodthirsty Islamists, but the Muslim Brotherhood. They weren't exactly open-minded, downright obtuse even, according to some, but good Muslims. They had a social role, as I had seen in Algeria. I still went to ask them if we could go and settle down. I chose one with a nice beard, just in case the solidarity between bearded men worked. He agreed, but told me to wait a little longer. We had patience. And we waited on the other side of the square, facing the old people sitting in front of the mosque. I made several requests, and each time they told us to wait.

After two hours, we understood[1]. We gathered our things and left. Heading for Alexandria. It was the most logical route to India.

Ouch! What had we done there? We're just trying to get out of the city, but the lo cals don't agree. They think we're Israeli spies. We're blocked by a dozen overex cited guys demanding to see our passports. Luckily, in each group, there's a calmer guy who has more influence over the others. He sends someone to get a uniformed cop who looks at the passports and tells the angry ones to calm down and go home. This happens to us five times in two hours. Annoying, but, well, we get through it anyway. We finally arrive on the road to Alexandria.

Alexandria. Net mender.

What a change! It's a big city by the sea. We see fishermen mending their nets. No apparent poverty. No overpopulation. A fresh, pleasant air blows gently off the sea. We immediately find a place to sleep. It's in a Catholic school on vaca-

---

[1] Or not, maybe it was enough to wait a little longer.

tion, we're on the platform in front of the blackboard in the chalk dust. It's not exactly comfortable, but we're not picky.

There, we are told that the border with Israel is closed. Too bad, I would have liked to go for a walk in a kibbutz. Here we are stuck. Since we cannot return to Libya, because of the poverty of the Egyptian traders, the only direction left is Sudan with the possibility of going through Port Sudan and going to Yemen.

We're not very happy about it. But we have no choice. During the day, we go around the shops with our miracle paper. We're a long way from matching our Libyan recipes. People aren't indifferent, far from it, but we can see they're broke. We find a stallholder who offers us a local bread, that is, without yeast, which we open and into which he stuffs beans with a red sauce. A delight. It's called fool. He tells us to come every day, and if we want, we can have something else. We accept with pleasure, but we settle for this excellent fool.

One of the first days, we returned home towards the end of the afternoon. We passed by a bookstore. In front of his shop, an extremely smiley individual greeted us and invited us to sit on the chairs next to him. On the sidewalk, he had set up a rack of terracotta jars, three stories high, filled with fresh water. He greeted everyone and invited passersby to drink some water. We watched them calmly refuse or accept.

He tells us something in Arabic that we don't quite understand. Just the word hashish. We answer yes with a smile. He gets up and opens the door to a small private path that must lead to his garden, behind our chairs. On a small table sits a homemade water pipe. It's a large jar, with a wide neck, three-quarters filled with water. It's closed by a large piece of rubber with two holes. Two bamboo tubes are housed inside, one that goes straight into the water and the other stays in the air. He cuts with his teeth a strip of golden Lebanese, one of those legendary hashish that I haven't had the chance to try yet. He places it in the middle of the bowl filled with water pipe tobacco, delicately surrounds it with tiny embers, and we smoke pure hash on a background of tobacco that doesn't have time to burn.

Wow! The slap is very strong, especially since we haven't smoked anything for over a month, at least. We go back to sit on the chairs in front of his shop. And we watch with a big, beatific smile as the people walk past us. Some drink a little

water. Others politely refuse. The bookseller isn't selling a single book. He doesn't give a damn. Neither do we. One of his friends arrives, and the four of us return to the small alley. Then it's his friend who takes out his hash. More golden Lebanese! The four of us go back to sit and watch, smiling, the people passing by. Simple happiness.
Throughout our stay the same scenario unfolds in the same way every day at the same time.

One day, while we were shopping, a group of kids started following us. They insistently asked us "what is your name?" Michel had the brilliant idea of replying: "David and Isaac!" And the kids took us for Israeli spies and started throwing stones at us. We were forced to take refuge in a shop where the "big brothers" managed to chase the kids away with buckets of water.

It is not the same model, but the same principle.

But after about a month, we have to make up our minds. We're not here to see the Egyptians pass by. We're going to say goodbye to our bookseller friend. Surprise!

7 years on the road

He's giving us an exact replica of his water pipe, and he and his friend have chipped in to give us a nice piece of golden Lebanese. We almost have a tear in our eye. They're in the same state as us. A lump in our throat.
The Benghazi students' magic paper shows its limitations in a poor country. But we still manage to get enough money to travel to Aswan by train.

Who has ever traveled on an Egyptian train? Those who have, in third class, may have fond memories of it. But not me. Nor Michel either. There are lots of people with goats, sheep, and chickens. During stops at the stations, we are invaded by vendors selling everything we can eat or drink cheaply.

Leaving Cairo, we see a pyramid and the Sphinx in the distance. It didn't occur to us to go and see them up close. In reality, we couldn't care less. We're not in Egypt for tourism; it's simply our route.

This train doesn't go fast, and to sleep, we lie down under the seats, among the pistachio seeds spat out by the passengers. It's very dirty, but we'll wash in Aswan. If the train ever gets there.

Finally, we discover Aswan. Where the equivalent of an atomic bomb is located: the dam inaugurated by Nikita Khrushchev and Gamal Abdel Nasser. All you have to do is blow it up, and all of Egypt ends up in the Mediterranean. What we see isn't inviting. The place is all yellow and full of dust. It's rather discouraging. Luckily, we discover that there are hotels for those who can afford them. So, not us. However, they are surrounded by beautiful, comfortable green lawns with small groves that provide shelter from prying eyes. There's a tap nearby. We go there and wash ourselves thoroughly. We wash our clothes and spread them out next to us. It's so hot that they'll dry overnight. And the big moment arrives: we're going to inaugurate the water pipe of our bookseller friend from Alexandria.

Ooh! This golden Lebanese is still as effective as ever. Once the pipe is washed and cleaned, we hide it under our drying clothes. And we lie down on this thick grass and look at the stars.

And I go back to my side, trying to merge, as I call this experience. I can't do it, but I feel a great happiness in my heart. This moment is almost magical. We have no worries. We enjoy this moment.

7 years on the road

Aswan has modernized.

Tomorrow will be a different story. We have a little money left, enough to take the steamer up the Nile, behind the dam, but nothing left to eat.

The steamer resembles a large metal barge where, instead of cargo, passengers are herded into the hold. I take a look and immediately back away. No way am I joining all these unfortunates crammed into this oven. It must be at least fifty de grees. The deck is empty because there are no safety devices. There are just two ventilation shafts facing each other. Two masts, in case of engine failure, are lying on them. Michel glances at me. We understand each other immediately. I place my blanket on the masts and Michel puts his sleeping bag underneath. This makes a tent for us, open on one side, which shelters us from the sun and we admire the dry, yellow desert bordering the Nile. Of course, we devote our time to the water pipe. Later we will learn that we have gone up the lake created by the dam, and not the Nile itself. We didn't know it, but we suspected it a little. Lake Nasser is very long and must contain piles of archaeological treasures stupidly drowned.

In the evening, people come out of the oven and come to cool off a bit. Among them are rather tanned Arabs and many Black people. They are the first we meet. They look scared and submissive. It leaves a strange impression.

7 years on the road

The first night, we slept right under the temple of Abu Simbel. It didn't occur to us to visit it, which would have been impossible from the lake anyway, especially at that hour. We spent a delightful night, as usual, under the stars.

Abu Simbel

Michel managed to find us something to eat. It's rice-based. We don't know exactly what it is. It's not to our taste, but we have no choice. We spend a second and third day in our small, smoky tent overlooking the yellow desert. And then, we fi nally arrive at the Sudanese border: at Wadi Halfa.

It's a tiny town, completely covered in sand, with a train station. Customs formal ities don't drag on with us. Always for the same reason.

We're not acting like amazed tourists, we're looking for the road to, perhaps, Port Sudan where we hope to find a boat that will take us to India.

Small problem, there isn't one. No road at all, no track, no trucks, nothing. There's only the train and it's a toll. A few bearded Americans with backpacks get out of the steamer. They were down there, in the oven, with the other passengers. We ask them for a little money, but they flatly refuse. So we decide to "burn the hard stuff," as our parents used to say. We climb into an empty cattle car heading back south. And there: a real mess. The suspensions are dead. We have to stand on tiptoe to cushion the shocks. We feel sorry for the cows who couldn't do it.

Wadi Halfa 70s

We ended up getting caught by the cops in a tiny town. We had gotten out of our wagon to get water. They took our passports and told us we had to pay a fine. We showed them our Koranic papers. But that wasn't enough. We went into the town to look for shops, but there weren't any. So we went to the market and collected a few coins, almost nothing. That was enough for the cops and they let us go. It must have been a matter of principle.

7 years on the road

Meroe Pyramids

7 years on the road

7 years on the road

From Sudan to Chad

Port Sudan! Or almost: we're on the road. Well, the problem is, there's no trail. Only tire tracks leading off in all directions. We wait two days, not far from a dried-up shrub. No one passes. We return the second evening to the village where this invisible trail begins.

We tour the trucks that are supposed to go to Port Sudan. The drivers camp. And then it works!

The Algerian Sahara is a refreshing stroll next to this corner of desert. The sun re ally beats down. I don't regret buying a second chèche—a turban. There are no Tuaregs here, but rather strange tribes. They wear a wooden comb in their hair. They don't have Negroid features, but they are still very black. They have skeletal cows, or zebus, that search for food on this arid ground. They all have a sword at their side and carry a spear, which they hold in their hands, across their shoulders. But they are smiling.

Port Sudan is a city similar to Alexandria, but much smaller. There's no apparent poverty. We settle down in the central square, relatively sheltered from the onlookers, on a thick English lawn. And here, I think of Henri de Monfreid, whose books I had so enjoyed when I was a teenager.

We decide to go see the port police to let us know when there will be a boat to Yemen. We're greeted by a cop, nice, except he's erased Israel with a knife on his big map of the Middle East. I'm a little blown away, because I didn't think it was that official.

We're going to take a walk around the harbor. There's a ship there that must be French, judging by the flag hanging from the end of its mast. We consult each other with a glance and climb aboard.
The crew is Breton. They all have a strong accent from the Douarnenez, Brest, or Paimpol areas.

7 years on the road

We are greeted with joy and when I tell them I am Breton, they go wild. "A Breton hippy!" they shout.

They pull out the front page of Ouest-France[1] announcing that Rennes has won a cup or a football championship. We immediately ask where the ship is going. It's going to Djibouti. It's not really our route, but it's also a port. The sailors are sorry and also tell us that the skipper, a Frenchman, isn't taking passengers.

One of them rushes to see the commander. But no. He has strict orders. It's a no. Period!

They are disappointed. Much more than us, because we are used to it. To make amends, they take out bottles and glasses. A Breton custom.

Black hole. I wake up on deck in a roll of ropes. Michel is still asleep, his head also resting on the ropes.
It's been a long time since we've had any alcohol. The crew says goodbye, and we make our way back down as best we can.

We'll stay a few more days, and if we don't find a boat, we'll try to get to Khartoum. The golden Lebanese is gone. We're not going to be able to buy any around here. There probably are some, but we don't know who to ask. And since we have no money, the problem is solved.

While waiting for a miraculous ship, we go around the shops again with our papers prepared by the Benghazi students. It's not working well. Very well.

And then, one morning, the population of Port Sudan gathers by the dozen around radios playing military music. It reminds me of the flea market in Saint-Ouen, when I bought my backpack and sleeping bag. People are nervous and anxious. A young man explains to us in international English—that is, the kind everyone speaks and understands, except native English speakers—that there's a coup d'état going on in Khartoum.

President Nimeiry, a dictator to be exact, managed to escape through his office window. And he counterattacked with his presidential guard.

---

[1] News-paper published in Brittany.

7 years on the road

In the evening, a procession forms. Judging by their appearance, the demonstrators are civil servants. They are all dressed in Western clothes. They support the coup. But there is no outpouring of joy. I join the manifestation, in my gandoura and we go around our square three times. Then they take another direction, I stop there and join Michel.
The next day, silence. Except for the military music blaring from the radios. In the late afternoon, a huge clamor comes from the poor neighborhoods.
It's kids running to the seafront. Each one carries a small twig with two or three leaves. They sing something like "Nimeiry ya, nam Nimeiry ya." The coup has failed. Smiles return. The news has replaced the military music.

Gaafar el Nimeiry

That said, we don't really feel concerned. We just hang out in the small park. We're in no rush.

After a week, we feel like going to the movies. It's never happened to us before. But this is special. They're showing "La Grande Vadrouille." De Funès and Bourvil have dubbed themselves into English. At the bottom of the screen, an Arabic translation scrolls from right to left.

2/22. *The Coliseum Cinema, Khartoum, in the year of its opening, 1935.* "Now playing" were "Les Miserables", "It Happened One Night", and "Peter Ibbetson". Owing to the climate, this was an open-air cinema. Patrons passed through the façade to walled, roofless seating. (Ref. A69/36. Collection: E.G. Sarsfield-Hall. Photographer: Karakashian.)

This is the cinema where we saw the film.

But before the film begins, we're treated to news reports from Khartoum. It's a bloodbath. The camera focuses on the rebels killed during the assault. It's really not a pretty sight. President Nimeiry seems resentful.
We decide to head for Khartoum and cross Africa to try our luck on the West Coast.

The road is completely broken. But we finally arrive in Khartoum. But we're not sure. It seems this city has two names: Khartoum and Umm Durman. In fact, Umm Durman seems to be the old name for Khartoum.

7 years on the road

We take a taxi. The first taxi of my life. And Michel says "Bongo!" to the driver, who hesitates for a second and takes off. In the Arabic dialect of the capital, it means "cannabis." It's the only word we know. He drops us off in a courtyard where about ten cars and bicycles are parked. A small adobe hut has a tiny window opening onto the courtyard. About fifteen people are patiently waiting their turn, queuing up. When ours arrives, he refuses to serve us. We try to explain in international English. Nothing works. Then, a young guy comes to our aid. He explains to the shopkeeper a lot of things we don't understand. In the end, he comes back with a big ball of grass full of resin. He offers it to us. We want to pay, but no, it's a welcome gift because he's putting us up at his place.

We accept and go with him to his family compound. The welcome is not exactly affectionate, but they are good Muslims and apply the rules of hospitality. The young man tells us his name is Abdel Ithnan, that is to say: son of - number Two. Seeing our bewildered expression, he explains that all the sons of the house are called Abdel and they have a number according to their arrival in this world. His older brother is called Abdel Wahad, that is to say: son of - number One.

He just got back, in an almost new car. He works for state television. He's a little depressed and prefers to talk to us another day. Well, in the end, we don't give a damn about any of the Abdels. The grass propels us into the stars. We sleep in the courtyard of the house on beds made of braided ropes on a wooden frame with legs.

The next day, we continued our search for money with the Arabic paper. It was starting to look a bit dull, but we still made a little money.

But what strikes us are the colorful posters showing the miraculously saved President. We obviously don't understand a word of what's written. In Arabic, I can only read Allah. A passerby explains to us in impeccable English that free and democratic elections are going to be held. When I ask him why, he replies that it's the moment for the President to test his popularity.

A few days later, Abdel Ithnan explained to us the rules for operating a polling station. There were two ballot boxes: a large one with a colored portrait of the president in full uniform, and a small black one with a large black register. This box was used to record the names and addresses of voters. There were also two types of ballots: one printed in color with the president's name and another blank. Of course, there were no other candidates.

Abdel Ithnan votes for the president. He explains to us that those who vote against Nimeiry will be in trouble. We have no doubt about it.

The vote count takes place that same evening. He wins hands down with a score of 98.78%. Abdel Wahad explains to us, once he gets home from work, that the few intellectuals or activists who voted in the black box have just been arrested. He's friendly, but sensitive. He shudders at the thought of going back to work the next day. He says goodbye and goes to bed.

We see him again a few days later. He is disgusted. Every day he witnesses thirty executions. Those who voted against Nimeiry are shot after being severely tortured. The executions are carried out one by one. In the presence, and to the great pleasure, of the dictator.

We decide to leave again. But where? Neither north, where we came from, nor to the east coast to reach Djibouti, where we would have to go through war-torn Eritrea, much less south where civil war is raging. We still have the West. If we can find a boat in Nigeria to circumnavigate Africa, and who knows, a way back to India?

We don't really believe it anymore. But we have to move on. It was about time, Abdel Ithnan's parents thought we were intruding a bit, and despite, or following, the rules of hospitality, they kicked us out. More precisely, we found our belongings, carefully stored, next to the compound door. On the outside. It's clear, and it avoids heartbreaking goodbyes.

We decide to head to Chad. We take the ticketless train to El Fasher, the capital of Darfur.

To escape the heat, we climb onto the roof of the train, like dozens of other passengers. What we hadn't noticed was that it was the rainy season. Torrential rain fell on us. We protected ourselves as best we could. It didn't last, and the sun came out again. And then, the yellow desert turned green. A whole host of small green and white flowers brightened up the new landscape. It was impressive.

7 years on the road

It's much better on the roof, except when it rains.

From the train, we move on to the trucks and during a stop, some villagers come to offer Michel and me a dish reserved for distinguished guests. Is it because we're foreigners or because we're white? In any case, their dish doesn't delight us. It's raw calf's liver—or sheep's, I don't know—with slices of raw onions, too. They have to insist heavily so that we swallow, without chewing, a piece of liver between lots of pieces of onion. I'm well aware that we're not behaving as we should, but raw liver...

Finally, we arrive at El Fasher. It's hardly a big city. In fact, there are two parts: the first, up a long, extremely steep hill, is the Arab and vaguely modern city. At the bottom of the hill, there's a huge shantytown crammed with Black people in appalling poverty. The only ones commuting are the Black kids who supply drinking water to the Arab city, which has no running water. The kids have a yoke on their shoulders that supports two twenty-liter cans. The Arabs give them a ridiculous amount of money in comparison to the effort they've made.

We ask a friendly shopkeeper who has just invited us for tea who these people are. He replies, "They are just Slavs." He says this with a contempt that truly shocks us.

For a moment, I consider going down the hill to see them. But its steepness puts me off. I'd have a lot of trouble getting back up. And then wisdom, let's call this feeling that, tells me not to go looking for trouble.

El Fasher, Sudan, 1971

While walking through the Arab town, we meet a friendly priest, French or Italian, I don't remember. He invites us to sleep as long as we like, near his church, in a garden protected by a high wall. Just on the other side, to the east, a mosque with a loudspeaker makes us jump. The priest laughs. Then

he reassures us. The call to prayer only takes place five times a day. I ask him what he thinks of this racism towards the Blacks down the coast. He has a hard time saying what's on his mind. They are animists and terrified of the Arabs. Before, the latter sold them as slaves to desert tribes, who in turn sold them to whites or other Arabs. He goes to see them from time to time. But it's very frowned upon, by the Arabs and the Blacks alike.

7 years on the road

After a few days, we're settled in El Fasher. We found a restaurant owner like in Alexandria who, of his own accord, offered to feed us every day for free. If we didn't know anything about the existence of Black people down the coast, and if we liked being woken up in the middle of the night by a loudspeaker, which should be called a loud-screamer, El Fasher would be a very nice place.
While shopping with our Quranic paper, we came across a photographer. He hadn't earned anything all day yet, so he offered to take a picture of us.

I sent the negative to my parents a few days later. It's the only photo I have from that time.

After about a month, we decide to leave. It's the rainy season. We hit the trail atop a truck, out of breath, something that will happen to us very often. The carriers don't heed the loading instructions. The passengers are perched atop a pile of various transportable items. We're heading for Chad. We'll find some French speakers; it'll be a change. And then, the former French colonies must have retained some of the good principles of France.

That's exactly it: The border is closed even though it's broad daylight! It's not time, a gigantic Chadian paratrooper tells us, the PM on his shoulder. He specifies that he doesn't like "black jackets.[1]"

It's starting well!

---
[1] Thugs.

7 years on the road

7 years on the road

Chad and Central African Republic

The next morning, the border opens. The imposing paratrooper isn't there. A white man in civilian clothes signals us to join him. In a low voice, he tells us that the road is closed at Abéché because of the rebels. We thank him, but we continue into Chad anyway.

Abéché is the first town coming from the east. A truck drops us off at the entrance. As we gather our belongings, a Jeep, or something similar, stops in front of us. Two white soldiers get out. Two Black men remain seated in front. They explain that the road is blocked by the rebels, and that they will take us by plane to Fort-Lamy, which was not yet called N'Djamena. They point to an unused, well-insulated cement building and explain that we must stay there and that they will take care of us. They ask for our passports and their eyes bulge. It's the Libyan visa that is having its effect. They leave, repeating that we must not stray far from this building.

It's hot, but very bearable. The problem is that we have to wait five days before the military offers us a plane ride to Fort Lamy. In the meantime, we have a little grass left, and we pass the time peacefully in the shade. The French soldiers—who are at home in Chad—bring us food. It's good, and we're happy with it. In the evening, we're invaded by mayflies who come to kill themselves on the building's oil lantern.

I learned later that the military had made inquiries everywhere, including the Saint-Brieuc gendarmerie[1]. It must be said that at the time, anyone who had spent a few weeks in Libya was necessarily an international terrorist.

The plane is a far cry from a 707. We sit in the paratrooper's seat. It's an old plane, and we hope it arrives intact. We didn't really take this rebel story seriously. In all the countries we traveled through, the only Westerners we met and stayed with were in Benghazi, Libya. The conversation never turned to a possible armed con

---

[1] The gendarmes are like police officers, but military.

flict. The two factions must have declared war on each other when we were in Egypt or Sudan.

It's dark when we arrive in Fort-Lamy. We look for a secluded spot to sleep. A square with a yellow lawn beckons.

1950. When N'Djamena was still called Fort-Lamy

The next day, we meet a bearded American. He's a member of the Peace Corps. It was Kennedy's idea. These volunteers mainly work the wells and pumps. It's always getting silted up. He invites us to his house. He lives there with another very hairy man. We restocked on weed—it should be noted that in sub-Saharan Africa you can find it everywhere and it costs practically nothing. We spend our time smoking. So do they. They're half-hippies. Probably very into religion. But we don't bring that up.

After a few weeks, we entered Fort Archambaud. Since then, the southern capital has been called Sarh. We found other "Peace Corps." They lived communally in a large house in a pleasant neighborhood with tall trees that were a welcome

7 years on the road

change from the dry yellow of the rest of the city. They employed several boys[1]. We were received rather well, as was the grass we bought in Fort Lamy.

The next morning, we stroll around town. The Chadian kids love the name of our president: Pompidou. They think it's a great name and pester us to tell them we love him. Michel sends more than one of them packing.

Our papers written in Arabic are in poor condition. So we decide to put on an exhibition of the horrors I drew in Rennes. We need a sidewalk for the magnificent "Help us continue our journey" in colored chalk.

But a police car, with two black cops, prevents us from going any further. The sub-prefect is waiting for us at his office. Oh? Okay, let's go. They take our passports. We climb into the jeep, and off we go, youth!

He makes us wait for half an hour. Since we're still high from our morning joint, it doesn't bother us.

An employee opens the door for us and bows obsequiously. The prefect is an unpleasant guy. He has a very high opinion of himself. He's wearing a wedding suit. He doesn't invite us to sit down, but we do anyway. We smile. We have nothing against him, and in principle, he has nothing against us.

We must be mistaken, because he looks down on us. He accuses us of not emphasizing our loyalty to Georges Pompidou. Michel tells him that he doesn't give a damn about Pompidou, and I tell him that I, as a Breton, am not concerned.

This drives him mad. He shows us through the window some small shacks, like toilets at the bottom of the garden. They have corrugated iron roofs. He tells us there are three Moroccans inside, one per shack, dying from the heat. There are no windows. He belches and threatens to make us share their fate. We don't believe it and continue to smile. So, he decides to expel us from Chad. Killing white people risks causing trouble.

---

[1] A "boy" is a boy of about ten years old who acts as a servant. There is one for the car, another for the garden, another for cleaning, etc.

7 years on the road

The African soldiers escorting us are very nice, as is the white man accompanying them, who must be their leader. We quickly dropped by the Peace Corps community to pick up our things. I tell them we'll see each other again soon. The soldiers don't care.

This short Jeep ride through southern Chad is highly enjoyable. Arriving at the large village, probably located on the border, the soldiers leave us, return our passports, and wish us a safe journey.

Little is known about the Central African Republic except that it is led by Jean-Bedel Bokassa. The famous Bokassa. He is a dictator whom France supports. Not willingly, unlike the others, but the interests at stake are enormous. The Bouar base in the west of the country is the nerve center of the French army, which dominates Africa. From there, all the countries of the African "Francophonie" can be reached very quickly.

Jean-Bedel Bokassa, president and brigadier general, on the left, emperor on the right.

Bokassa replaced David Dako in a coup d'état on New Year's Eve. It became a national holiday. He was a second lieutenant in the French army. He is a brigadier general in the Central African army. He would become emperor under the name Bokassa the First.

He immediately imposed his "brand." This is summed up in his propaganda posters. They are in two parts. On the left, we see his ministers in small black and white photos. They are all writing diligently in a school notebook. And on the right, a magnificent color portrait of Bokassa in full uniform, wearing all his decorations, right down to the hem of his jacket, and staring into the camera, his eyes fierce and conquering.

As you get closer, you can see the name of each minister and their ministry. Nothing exciting, except that Jean-Bedel combines his position as president with all the strategic ministries: Prime Minister, Chief of the Armed Forces, Minister of Defense, Minister of the Interior, Minister of Finance, and many others...

There are plenty of legends about him. His nickname is Kourou, which means "doesn't give a damn about death," according to what we're told. He has the right of the first night over the wives of ministers and comes alone at night to pay his respects to the woman he likes. The husband can only let this happen, otherwise his future becomes rather bleak...

Finally, we land at Kilometer Five. This is the name of the neighborhood located five kilometers from the city center. It will turn into a butcher's shop in 2015 between Muslims and Christians. It is located practically exclusively in the shade of mango trees. It is, theoretically, the most disreputable neighborhood in Bangui. Cassava alcohol: Tako, premium weed: M'Bako, pretty and friendly "little brothels" – prostitutes, open-air nightclubs. We hear music every night.

Our first encounter is with Oscar the Great. He speaks impeccable French. He gives us the right information on weed and alcohol vendors. It's not expensive at all. The cassava alcohol isn't particularly good. It's even difficult to drink, but it packs a punch. The weed, on the other hand, is top-notch.

This is the neighborhood where the thugs live, and they're pretty nice, it must be said. In the morning, they take the bus to the city center, picking passengers' pockets. They come home when they have enough for a 33 cl bottle of cassava alcohol and a banana: that's the name given to the dose of weed because of its shape. They smoke a single, pure joint in the late afternoon and go hunting for "little brothels"—young girls who do "shop my ass."

We met an uprooted Senegalese man who could only smoke in paper from "Dakar Matin," the daily newspaper to which he subscribed.

7 years on the road

A fairly high-ranking official rents us a one-room hut. His name is Benoît and he enjoys our company. He comes over from time to time in the evening with a bottle of wine. We talk about everything, but especially about Bokassa.

The thugs are nice to us. They have a single pair of perfectly creased trousers that they iron every day, a single pair of shoes gleaming with shoe polish, and one or two shirts with a breast pocket for cigarettes.

Their joints are "deadly." Twenty centimeters long! Each of them smokes their own. They drink a small bottle of Tako, and in the evening, they have to drink a few beers and bring home a nice "little brothel." This is the usual routine of the neighborhood thugs.

Oscar the Great is not one of them. He was born in Kilometer Five. His mother sells Tako and M'Bako.

Benoît always wears a suit when he comes to our house. He's a pure soul. He only collects his salary from time to time, but refuses any corruption. He won't last long. Someone will want his job and accept the bribes.
We listen to the radio a lot in Bangui. Bokassa makes unscheduled appearances and monopolizes the microphone. I heard him appoint himself a Lieutenant General. It went something like this: "By decree of 8 slash 08 slash 1971 - Major General Jean-Bedel Bokassa is appointed Lieutenant General as of this day. Signed, the President of the Republic, Jean-Bedel Bokassa."

Michel and I laugh about it, but not all Africans.

One day, I'm talking to a very annoyed guy. He plays in a modern African music band. His band isn't rich, but it's good. One day, he and his musicians are summoned by Bokassa. He tells them he's paying for them to go to France to better train in music, he's paying for the best possible equipment, but in exchange, they must call themselves "the Little Bokassas" and must only sing songs glorifying him. Needless to say, they can't refuse.

We really like Kilomètre Five; it has a little paradisiacal side. We've only seen that side, but we assume there's another, much less pleasant side. Oscar, known as the Great, explained to us how taxes work in Bokassa's country. Since people

7 years on the road

don't have any official or regular income, they have to buy a sticker every year and keep it with them in case of an inspection. Those who don't have one are sent to a presidential cotton plantation in the north of the country, far from everything, about 100 km from the nearest village. There have been very few successful returns, including one we meet.

That morning, someone knocked on our door rather forcefully. I went to open it, still sleepy. A soldier looked at me, then apologized and closed the door. I opened it again, and there I saw the less pleasant side of the area. Kilometer Five was surrounded by the army with several trucks. Anyone who couldn't produce the sticker was crammed inside. Oscar was lucky.

We decide to leave. We thank Benoît and the next day we head to Cameroon where we hope to find a boat in Douala.

For a change, we're picked up by a car. A Land Rover, in very good condition. The driver is a big black man who talks a lot. He explains that he's a minister of who knows what. He tells us how much he thinks of Bokassa and his cotton policy.

After a while, he stops in front of a bar in the middle of the countryside and invites us for a beer. A Mocaf, the local beer. In fact, it's not a bistro but a dance hall where couples warmly embrace on the dance floor. Our driver doesn't mince words, goes up to one of the couples, separates them, and starts dancing with the woman under the dismayed gaze of her ex-partner, who says nothing and leaves.

It seems obvious to me that this dance hall, by day, I should add, is more of a brothel than anything else. We decide to leave. Our driver has forgotten us and is obsessed with his dancer. We leave them there and head back on the road, toward Cameroon.

Unfortunately, visas are limited to ten days. It's a bit tight to find a boat. So, we decide to head back to Chad, from where we'll try to enter Nigeria. In Lagos, it's possible we can find a ship that circumnavigates Africa.

We return to see our American friends at Sarh — Fort-Archambaud — hoping that our friend the sub-prefect will leave us alone.

7 years on the road

Along the way, we come across a rather special café. It's a guy who set up shop just before a river, in the middle of the countryside. There's no house, no table or chair, but a small fire on the ground. Over it, he boils water and delicately pours it into small metal balls with long necks, into which he adds a ball of dry straw to make a filter. We see, on the fire, a small metal plate on which coffee beans are roasting. He explains to us with a gesture that these beans, once crushed, are put into the long-necked balls before adding water. He gives us each a cup and we pour the mixture, filtered through the straw, into it. It's really very good, and we enjoy it.

And then we continue on our way, very satisfied with this original coffee.
We enter without any problem through the border where we had been expelled[1]. The friends from the Peace Corps community are rather reserved. But since we bring good grass, it's okay. Still feeling a certain unease, I ask the chief friend what's going on. He explains to me that after our departure, the sub-prefect summoned him. He said all sorts of bad things about us. The worst offense was entering his office with a banana in our hands. We allegedly peeled it and threw the skin on the floor, on his carpet. Obviously this is completely false and we burst out laughing. But I can see that the head of the community, which in principle doesn't have a leader, believes the sub-prefect and not us.

We don't like these "Peace Corps," and we leave early the next day to try to enter Nigeria.

---

[1] But which doesn't have a border post with cops and customs officers.

7 years on the road

Nigeria - Gabon and a little prison

To enter Nigeria, a gigantic and already crazy country, we have to go through Cameroon. Here, it's the same as last time: we're given a ten-day visa. That's enough for us to go to Nigeria, where widespread corruption prevents us from passing. We should be able to bribe people at every entry point, but, well... We arrive in Maiduguri, which will become Boko Haram's stronghold in the 21st century. But we can't go any further. It's the first time this has happened to me since I set foot in Africa. We don't have a single cent on us, and the customs officers won't let us pass. So we return to Chad, grumbling. We go back through Cameroon and its ten-day visas.

In a small town, we buy five "banana fingers" of grass[1]. It's very resinous grass compacted into the shape of a large banana and wrapped in banana leaves. It costs almost nothing. With that, we have enough to last us for a good while. Michel is the one who carries them.

A truck drops us off in a slightly larger town with a paved road. It's a bit of a change from the laterite track that literally transforms us into Red-Skins. And then all of a sudden, we see cops on the sides. It looks like a convoy is going to pass by. We continue walking in the middle of the road, since there's no traffic. And then, one of the cops comes towards us. Identity check. I feel a little pang in my heart thinking about the "five banana fingers" in Michel's bag. But no, we're not in France. He takes a look at our passports and greets us. He tells us that a convoy of officials is going to pass by and wishes us a good trip.

We hit the road again, but we don't want to see Sarh again. So we go down to Garoua and turn off towards Bouar in the Central African Republic. Strange, there's no traffic. We have to walk for three days eating only unroasted peanuts and pineapples. This diet suits us fine for two days, but on the third, I don't want it anymore.

---

[1] For 100 CFA francs, which correspond to 15 euro cents.

7 years on the road

An obese white man found us on the road and took us to his house. He's a construction manager and is responsible for keeping the trails in good condition. There's just one problem: he has no budget.

At first glance, we see that his marriage is unhealthy. He married a beautiful Black woman who openly despises him. The situation is awkward. She makes thinly veiled allusions to us. He pretends not to notice. So do we.

That evening, during dinner, we talk about Bokassa, of course. I suddenly realize that she must have slept with the dictator. Which would have generated the contempt she has for her husband. But I don't know if it's because she's proud of his achievement or because she can't forgive him for not intervening.

They tell us about the president's visit to a construction site. Since our host can't afford to hire employees, he's asked for prisoners to do the job. The "volunteer" inmates are chained up, which reminded me of the Sam Cooke song "Chain Gang."

Bokassa and the fat white man are sitting under an awning, leaning against an empty tanker truck. They are calmly drinking a beer when a prisoner tries to escape. He is immediately recaptured. The dictator, who has more than a few beers in his belly, lectures him. The prisoner kneels down and asks "sorry, Dad"—the only phrase Bokassa likes.

After a few blows from the presidential cane, he was thrown into the empty cistern, which was heated to white-hot in the sun. He took several hours to die, to the great joy of his executioner and the great discomfort of the white man.

Kilometer Five has lost some of its liveliness. The big roundup has seriously depopulated the neighborhood. Oscar the Great is still there. He takes us to a wise man who sells top-quality weed. Night has just fallen in his compound. A radio station is playing local African music. It's very pleasant, even if we don't understand a word. Suddenly the music stops. And Bokassa's voice, heavily drunk, rises in French. His message is addressed to Indira Gandhi. He implores her not to attack Pakistan. He tells her she is as courageous as Joan of Arc. He asks for forgiveness on behalf of mankind, he cries... And it goes on for a very, very, very long time.

7 years on the road

We end up leaving with Oscar. He tells us a story that could be true, at least in part. Bokassa believes he is the son of General de Gaulle. His mother supposedly worked in a hotel where he was passing through and had a sexual relationship that led to the clandestine birth of little Jean-Bedel, who, however, is not mixed race.
At the general's funeral, he reportedly lay down on the coffin, shouting "Daddy." Whether this is true is unknown, but it's possible. He must have been very drunk.

We would have liked to stay and catch our breath a bit, but we're still on the road to India. So we're heading to Gabon. But to get there, we still have to go through Cameroon and its ten-day visas.

Somewhere along the road, we are invited to the home of a missionary priest. He's a young, white, long-haired biker. He's a big hit with his young parishioners. He invites us to eat. He has guests: white nuns. We drink sacramental wine. A sweet white wine, not very pleasant. We hit the road again after the meal.

Finally, we arrive at the top of Gabon, among the Fangs. We are invited to stay for a few days with a coffee and cocoa producer. For the coffee he drinks, he buys canned Nescafé[1] at the grocery store in the neighboring village.

Our host is a Jehovah's Witness. He has a problem. He's married, and his wife wants him to take another wife so she can share the workload. But that's forbidden in his religion. He asks us for advice. We're very embarrassed. Finally, we tell him to listen to his wife.

The local herb is full of resin and quickly propels us into bliss. Michel makes one of the best joints he's ever made. He rolls the herb directly into a piece of fresh to bacco leaf, which sticks perfectly.

We have a problem with Central African food. We can't get used to cassava ball, using the leaves as vegetables. So we ask our host to cook for ourselves in the hut he's made available to us. It's not very nice, but he understands and asks his wife to provide us with vegetables and peanuts.

---

[1] Coffee powder.

7 years on the road

One evening, after I'd just cut a tiny chili pepper, I automatically ran my hand through my jeans, where the sweat was dripping, even though the day was already over, and there: a gigantic burn, I started jumping around in front of our host, his family, and his friends, who were dying of laughter. After a while, it passed. And then, Michel, who had taken over the cooking while I was jumping around, wiped a drop of sweat above his eye. And it was his turn to jump. But it was worse, and the Fangs were forced to put charcoal powder in his eye. It worked. This tiny chili pepper was the hottest I'd ever known.

Dried Iboga roots.

We're almost at the equator. The jungle is dense and the heat is humid. There are tons of midges, mosquitoes, and other pests that cling to our skin. It's very unpleasant.

Arriving in a very shady village, we stand at the exit, ready to give a thumbs-up. No one passes by. The owner of the last house invites us for a drink. Okay, let's go. Next to the house, there's a large wooden shed that looks new. He tells us that's where "Bwiti[1]" is practiced. We've already heard about it. Oscar the Great explained it to us, but we didn't believe it. These are people who eat a powdered Iboga root, to the beat of completely crazy drum rhythms. They enter a trance, and some of them communicate with their ancestors. The officiants wear a green chasuble with a green cross on the back. Okay, now we believe it. Maybe not

---
[1]Pronounce booti.

contact with the ancestors, but a hallucinogenic trance, yes. Like young Westerners with LSD and Mexican Indians with peyolt.

Meanwhile, Michel, the off-roader roller, makes a joint. We pass it around. Before it's finished, our host starts acting strange. The whites of his eyes turn bright red, and then I sense danger. Michel saw it too. We grab our things, say goodbye, and head back out onto the trail, not exactly reassured.

We have trouble finding a truck that will take us. They don't believe us when we tell them we don't have a penny. There are kids who think we're monks or missionaries because of my beard. We still find one that goes to Libreville.

Libreville, a city that is misnamed.

It's really a big city, in the European way. The contemptuous looks from the whites worry me a little. We run into young French people leaving in 2CV[1]s. They're construction site managers. They don't know anything about it, but the whites don't want to see someone of the same color as them doing a black man's job. The whites have to "set an example." So, rather than seeing a white man make cement, we offer him a job as a manager of some kind. They tell us they'll look for one for us. We kind of agree, but not completely. We have absolutely no desire to work. Work isn't really our thing. We're on our way to India, not to settle

---

[1] A car for the poor.

down. Even if it pays well. And what's more, being around white people who give lessons doesn't delight us at all.

We don't say anything, but we think it very strongly.

The next morning, we were going to hold an exhibition of my horrors on one of the sidewalks in Libreville. Immediately, several Black people stopped and talked with us. They all gave us a few coins. We talked about a lot of things.
I leave for a moment to buy something, and on my way back to our corner I pass a post office. There are a lot of people waiting in line at a counter, including a white woman about fifty years old. She's sulking. I give her a little friendly nod, thinking she's tired of waiting in line. Big mistake. She turns to me and yells, "Aren't you ashamed? You should set an example."
Oh dear, danger! I'll leave her to her curses. It smells bad, and we'll have to get out of this town.

When I return to where we exhibit my horrible drawings, Michel still talks with the young Gabonese people, but from time to time a white man passes by and acts as if we don't exist. The blacks harangue a couple, telling them that they should help their brothers, that they are selfish. Michel and I look at each other. It is urgent to pick up everything and clear out. Too late! The cops arrive and take us away.

It was quick. Gabon is really much worse than all the other countries Michel and I have traveled through, and even those I visited alone in 1969. There must be a lot of money to be made for the little whites and the big whites.
White bastards! I hate them! Descendants of slave traders! Teaching them lessons! They are the same people who denounced the Jews during the German nazi occupation. In Gabon, they are the oil kings[2], in France they are nothing. I am disgusted.

The commissioner is white, logical, and naturalized Gabonese, also logical, he lectures us. Always the same thing, whites must set an example for blacks. He sends us straight to the Libreville prison. We are charged with vagrancy and beg ging. Yes!

---

[2] If I dare say…..

7 years on the road

The prison's entrance courtyard is a small marvel. It should serve as an example for French prisons. That's what we say to ourselves upon entering. However, we have no idea what happens inside. We are greeted by two white men in uniforms of some unknown kind. They welcome us rather kindly. A black "trusted inmate" asks the chief why we are there. The white man replies that it's because we didn't arrive in a Mercedes. We are given the VIP area with the corrupt politicians. Why? Because we are white.

The VIPs are Blacks plus two or three Whites. There's the Bishop of Libreville, the postmaster, and five or six others, including one or two ministers and two or three secretaries of state. We don't know what they're accused of, and we don't try to find out. We settle into a small, unoccupied communal cell. There are no beds; it's a large wooden space where four or five people can lie down. We quickly become friends with the bishop. We do a little yoga. I know a few postures that I'd dug out of a manual. We read everything we can find. For me, it's the Koran. It can't be complete because it's a small book I have in my hands.
How repetitive! After a few pages I understand that we have to wage war on the infidels, because it appears all the time.

Today, it's a big meeting with the commander—white—in chief. All the prisoners are lined up two by two behind the cell chief. The white chief gives us a speech that we listen to only distractedly. He talks about honor, pride, atonement for one's sins... And then he points at us and tells us to approach. We go there quietly. It's at least a hundred meters, but he waits. As we pass, I see the Blacks looking at us, their eyes bulging. And then I think to myself that it's convenient to be a White. A Black man would have been massacred if he had done the same thing. Once we arrived, he smiled kindly and asked us if we had our high school diploma. Michel had one, so he appointed him teacher. I didn't, so I became head of the tool department. That's it, break it off.

One of the two or three white VIPs is the head of tools and will be released in a few days. He explains the job to me. In the morning, when the work crews go clearing outside the prison, he gives them each a machete. They have to be counted, but not in the evening when they come back. I don't know why we wouldn't count them. That's all. Nothing else to do.

7 years on the road

One of the guys who runs the kitchen has all his teeth sharpened to points. According to the others, he comes from a cannibal tribe. But that's not why he's here. He wanted to sleep with his sister-in-law. She didn't want to. So he killed her and fucked her while she was still hot. Other than that, he's a very nice guy. Michel and I eat well. When we entered, we were asked if we were on a diet. In Marseille, I understood the trick. You have to be vegetarian. So they make us litle dishes. With fried eggs, for example. The others, except for the VIPs who can buy prepared meals, eat cassava with a piece of meat one day and fish the next. For everyone else, it's only at lunchtime. There's nothing in the evening. One meal a day, that's all.

In my yoga studies, I learned how to eat to feel satisfied with almost nothing. It's quite simple: just chew until everything in your mouth is liquid. So, Michel and I became great chewers.

The commander-in-chief has trained the black prisoners in the iron discipline he endured as a child. Before entering, the cell leaders shout: "Life in a castle?" The response is: "As long as it lasts!" Then he asks: "Ideal?" The others respond: "Submission!" It's fun!
When new black prisoners arrive, they are systematically beaten by the guards, also black. Those who refuse to comply receive a special punishment: they must stare at the Gabonese flag in the full sun until they fall.

We also learned that on the day of our arrival, Albert-Bernard Bongo, who was not yet called Omar, gathered all the elite of Libreville to celebrate his third billion. We don't know if it was CFA francs or dollars.

One of the black VIPs explains to us how corruption works. It starts at the top of the pyramid, in the ministries. As soon as there's a new minister, he immediately receives requests for meetings from white salespeople selling luxury goods: Mercedes, swimming pools, a new house in Libreville and another permanent one in his home village. So the minister looks at how his colleagues live. They have everything. So he tells himself there's no reason why he shouldn't have anything. His salary is comfortable, so he can take out a loan. But the salespeople want a little cash to consolidate orders. So the minister looks in the ministry's slush fund. It's empty. His predecessor swiped everything before giving him the job. He's ashamed of not being able to cope, and so he accepts any sum of money from anyone with very ministerial eagerness. And he doesn't have to wait long. The corrupt solicitors are falling over themselves to give him money.

Albert-Bernard Bong

And the pyramid does the rest. Money flows in from everywhere, and civil servants are no longer paid, the roads remain dirt, and the people endure in silence. And France continues to reign, offering its immense humanism to the Gabonese people who didn't ask for so much.

We were quickly summoned to court, which gave us a two-month prison sentence. You guessed it, the judge, who was black, was the wife of the police commissioner, who was white! We weren't given a court-appointed lawyer. We weren't even offered one.

And then, time passes. I take the opportunity to finish reading the Quran, one of the few interesting books in the prison library, and we finish our two months. But, a slightly unpleasant surprise awaits us: as foreigners, we are locked up, awaiting repatriation, in a collective dungeon under the central police station. Of course, without trial or anything like that. But, it allows us to discover the screams of Black people being tortured on the floors. The land of human rights in all its splendor!

7 years on the road

There are about ten inmates who have completed their sentences waiting to be deported to their home countries. Some of them are from Equatorial Guinea. For them, it's certain death. It must be said that their president, Marcos, has gone completely mad. He seized all the country's money, which he stashed in metal army canteens. In exchange, he distributes vouchers to be exchanged for food, oil for lamps, and salt. The people are suspect of everything. Field work is collectively carried out by chained peasants, guarded by unpaid soldiers. Furious madness.
We ask them all how long they've been there. The record is one year. We're not excited.

They bring us the day's meal: a can of sardines and a limp baguette. That's all, and it's like that every day. Luckily, one of the inmates has tinkered with a can opener that he hides under his mattress, otherwise you would have had to be resourceful to get to the sardines. Or have good teeth[1].

The French consul comes to see us and asks what we need. We tell him: our freedom. We have served our sentence. He tells us that if our family pays for the plane ticket to repatriate us, it won't be a problem. We refuse his offer. In reality, the whites don't want us hanging around in Gabon.
After a while, we realize that we won't get out of there easily. So, we decide to go on hunger strike, for our freedom and that of the other inmates who agree with us.

Big commotion at the central police station! White people on hunger strike, followed by others arbitrarily detained! If this gets out in Europe, it could look bad.

But for our fellow inmates, not eating is the worst thing they can do. Their strike will last half a day. Michel and I are summoned to the upper floors of the police station.

We arrive before a young black inspector. We smile, as usual. He takes it very badly. He accuses us of leading the other prisoners, of exerting pressure to start a revolt.

---

[1] To open the can. Africans of the time loved to open their beer with their teeth, and to open cans of sardines too.

7 years on the road

For once, he has white people as prisoners, even if it's completely illegal, and he'd like to take advantage of it. We understand that, but we'd like to get out of this cell. All of this, of course, has nothing to do with our smiles. Because we're always smiling. And that annoys him. Finally, he makes us return to the collective cell. Two hours later, the consul is back. He's completely shaken up. He makes us understand that we're lucky to be white. He actively works to get us sent back to the border.

We're happy, not only because we're getting out of our cells, but also because we've discovered the weak point in the legal system of Gabonese Françafrique: the hunger strike. We explain this carefully to our fellow inmates. But I can see they won't be overzealous. Food is too important in Africa.
A month later, we're free. It's been a long wait, though. We arrive during the day, transported in a Gabonese police Land Rover, within sight of the Cameroonian border post. And yes, Cameroon again. A formal exchange between the two police forces. The Gabonese, as stiff as a court, hand our passports to the only Cameroonian police officer present, sign several documents, and leave.

Immediately, the Cameroonian cop bursts out laughing and gives us back our passports. He says all the bad things he thinks about the Gabonese people and offers us a beer. Hot. We don't care, we drink it anyway. And he stamps our passports. Ten days. As usual!

We set off again on foot. Fed up with Africa. We admit we were completely wrong. Visiting Cameroon or Chad won't get us to Goa, Bombay, or Banares.

We are discussing what to do next. We were completely mistaken. The route to India passes through Europe. The route generally taken is this: Italy, Greece, Turkey, Iran, Afghanistan, Pakistan, India.

We're fed up with Africa. We have nothing against black people, except those who want to play white by spitting on their cultures and families, but we no longer want to go to jail, nor cross the borders of Cameroon with its 10-day visas.

Once we arrived in Chad, things were much better. The whites were soldiers who kept to themselves; they didn't try to "set an example." We don't know if the war is still going on in the east of the country.

7 years on the road

We decide to go around Lake Chad to the east, reach Niger, go back up to Agadez, cross the Sahara, and reach the Algerian coast. Michel wants to go to Morocco, but I'm worn out and tired. A return to Brittany would do me good.

7 years on the road

From Cameroon to Morocco

In Cameroon, in a middling village, Michel and I get stopped by the cops. It's an identity check. They're friendly and happy to check on white people. The police station has a large courtyard in front with a one-room hut, right at the entrance. About fifteen Black people, including a young, pretty woman, are waiting. They're all trembling with fear. The friendly cops are certainly less friendly with their compatriots. Screams of pain come from the small hut, and after about twenty minutes, a young guy comes out, his shirt ripped down the back and soaked in blood. The cop, a mountain with the face of a brute, who has just tortured him appears at the door of the hut, a piece of green garden hose in his hand. He signals to another of the future tortured to come join him. This one goes as if he were going to his death. The cop's screams are followed by the screams of the young guy. After a quarter of an hour, the tortured man comes out in tears and blood. The thick brute signals to the woman to join him. We can guess her fate. We hear a few screams and then a long silence. Tortured and raped. It's not good to be a woman in the hands of a torturer of any color.

We are tired of Africa. The divisions of countries do not correspond to anything natural. The Whites came to plunder the riches of the Blacks. The English were content with pillaging, contemptuous of the natives, while their French colleagues felt obliged to instill in them the "values of France" without taking into account their own, which resulted in a gigantic and lamentable fiasco. From our ancestors the blond, blue-eyed Gauls to the "fête-nat[1]" as a first name for those born on July 14, if it had not been tragic for the African peoples, it would have been comical.

We decide to go back up to Chad, skirt the lake of the same name, enter Niger, and head back up to Agadez. From there, we take a short trip across the Sahara, without any German-Greek epic. Michel hasn't experienced that, but as far as I'm concerned, I have no desire to encounter amateurs again.

After a quick stop in N'Djamena, we head north.

---
[1] National holiday, as it is written on the post office calendars.

7 years on the road

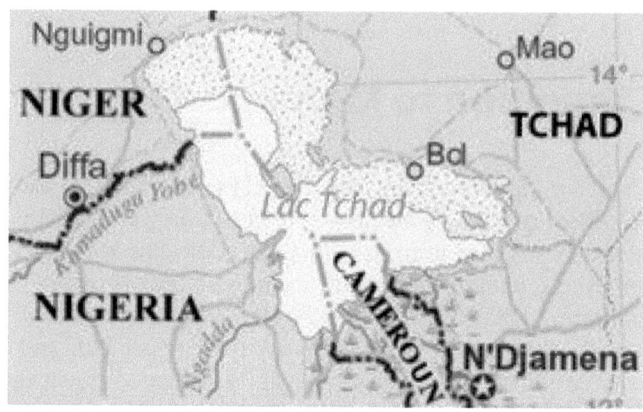

Well, there's a track in the sand, but the tire tracks go in all directions. We don't know which way is right, but there's one track that's clearer than the others. It's the right one, we assume. There's almost no traffic, but that's not the kind of detail that's going to change our minds. Every now and then a truck takes us a little further, but we're not moving forward.

There, in front of us, is a solid structure. It's at the edge of the runway. We put our things down at the foot of this building and climb up onto the roof, which serves as a terrace where there seems to be someone.

He's a white man. A soldier. He greets us almost with a smile. We are welcome in his fort. He serves in the French army and has been placed at the disposal of the Chadian army. He reigns over a troop of five or six Chadian volunteers. He has no illusions: if the northern rebels, supported by Libya, want to attack him, his few volunteers will immediately switch sides with their weapons. And he will climb onto the roof with a crate of grenades and try to hold out as long as possible.

It's cheerful! He brightens up for a few seconds when I tell him I'm Breton. He's from Paimpol[1]. He'd love to get back to the sea air, but he's not kidding himself. He offers us a warm beer.
After a while, we leave him to his tragic fate, and go towards our own.

---
[1] Like my mother.

7 years on the road

There are plenty of small towns along the lake, which is a few kilometers from the track. But seeing the lake doesn't interest us. I'm becoming increasingly unpleasant. Michel is much cooler. I can't stand hanging around this hill anymore. I left for India and I'm hanging around miserably in this desert. I admit I took the wrong road. I wasted a lot of time going around in circles. It's annoying me and I'm frankly in a bad mood. Michel is paying the price. This desert is so long, where even trucks don't venture. Okay, what I'm saying is a bit false; you can still find a few. But what a stupid idea to try to go around Lake Chad [1]!

And we arrive in a village, slightly different from the others. It's the inhabitants who change. They're black! So, unless we've turned the wrong way, we're in Niger. That's good news! Okay, there's no border post, but in Niger, the inhabitants of the south are black, while those in Chad at the same latitude are Arabs. We're welcomed like VIPs and they offer us pastis in the middle of the afternoon, while the sun beats down like a thick brute.

Actually, it's not pastis, but eau de cologne. One part for two parts water. It's not fifty-one, but seventy degrees. Everyone is drunk, but smells good. It's disgusting to drink. So we take a nap in the shade of a mango tree to celebrate our arrival at the exit gate of Black Africa.

The next morning, I wake up and shake out my blanket. And then, a scorpion falls out. We slept together!

The road to Zinder is long but relatively busy. We're glad to be on the road to North Africa. Since I'd already been there, in the other direction, on my first trip, I'm happy to be on familiar ground. We can build a simple but effective plan. Next stop: Agadez and its Tuaregs, Tamanrasset in Algeria, and Algiers. Then we'll see.
And above all, don't embark with Westerners. We need an Algerian truck that can cross this desert of dunes in three days.

But we stay a few days in Zinder, which offers no tourist attractions, aside from its meat market. The two- or three-year-olds amuse themselves by teasing the vultures perched on the market walls, ready to pounce on the meat stuffed with

---

[1] Now it has to go faster, the lake has dried up considerably.

fly droppings. Enough to make even the most bloodthirsty butcher a vegetarian. All that's missing is some Sergio Leone music for ambiance.

We're shaking ourselves off. The sooner we leave Zinder, the sooner we'll get closer to India, even if the difference is difficult to see.

So we head towards Agadez and are careful not to get into a Western 4x4. We need an Algerian truck.
We finally arrive in the Tuareg capital. We start looking for our trans-Saharan truck. We find a few. But we're more struck by the number of Western vehicles ready to brave the desert. There are a few who show off and act tough, real adventurers. The Land Rovers line up in front of the city's only hotel for Westerners.

Agadez.

That said, with Algerian trucks, we have a handicap. We have to pay. Not much, probably, but pay nonetheless. We feel we should work because our Koranic papers are now just a memory and I have no more horrors to expose[1]. And in Agadez, that wouldn't have worked at all. There isn't a single cement sidewalk!

---

[1] I don't remember how I lost them.

7 years on the road

We need to find a job for a day or two to pay for our passage. Real work, in this sandy village. The city center isn't huge, but the concessions[1] stretch as far as the eye can see all around. We should be able to find a job without too much difficulty. In Libreville, our heads were shaved when we entered the prison. So our hair is reasonably short, and my beard hasn't really grown out too much yet. We're presentable for work. However, we're not thrilled about it. Not at all! Any way, we'll have to do it. Unless we find another solution. We decide, early this evening, to meet with the French consul and ask him to find us some kind of job.

We find him easily. He's with his wife and a few friends in his garden, enjoying the mild evening temperature. They must be busy having a drink and probably smoking a joint. As soon as we arrive along the small path that leads to his house, the consul quickly comes to meet us, cutting us off. I imagine his wife throwing herself on the bundle of weed and hiding it on her.

We're a little amused, but we act as if we haven't detected anything. I explain the situation to him, that we need a job, anything, even a car washer. He stops us right away. "Come tomorrow at eight o'clock, I'll find you a truck going back to Algeria."

Always this need for a "positive" image of white people compared to black people: white people cannot do basic manual work. Even for a pot-smoking consul.

We find a fairly discreet spot where we lie down. Michel burrows into his sleeping bag, and I into my blanket. It's a very thick Army blanket that resists stones. And then the big unpleasant surprise begins. We are invaded by large, aggressive mosquitoes that manage to bite me more than once through the blanket. Big mos quitoes at the gateway to the desert! I wonder where they come from. But I end up falling asleep anyway.

The next day, we ride in the back of the truck. It doesn't have a huge load. There are no other passengers but us. An apprentice, called a greaser, is in the cab. That's all. The driver is sulking. He doesn't like being forced onto us. We don't have a water bottle. At the start, he pointed out a barrel full of water for us. We just take enough to drink. Ouch, hot water! I show Michel how to cool off with yogic breathing. We wedge the tip of our tongue between our teeth and breathe

---

[1] A concession (compound) is a local house with a large yard, surrounded by low walls.

through our mouths. When evening comes, the water from the barrel is refreshing. And we recover what we've sweated out.
We now know that those who always advised us to wait until evening to drink were right. During the day, it's pointless. Water turns into sweat. It's a waste of a scarce resource.

After the Nigerian border, where the gazelle barbecue had burned with a tire during my first crossing, we find the freshly paved Algerian track. It doesn't take long for us to arrive in Tamanrasset. Black Africa is far away. Phew! El chemz—the sun—is a little less harsh.

We slowly head back towards Algiers. The temperature drops gently and we quickly arrive on the Algerian coast.
We part ways. Michel, who has changed his mind, wants to go home right away, and I want to spend some time in the Rif, where all Moroccan cannabis grows, before returning home. Our adventure ends there. No heartbreaking goodbyes. Our relationship was on the rocks, as they say. All I can think about now is going to India; everything else is of no interest to me.

So I go to Ketama. It's the capital of kif[1]. From there, I'm told to go to Tleta-Ketama. It's a small village surrounded by terraced plantations. Only cannabis grows there.

Cannabis field near Ketama

---

[1] Kif is the name for cannabis in Morocco.

7 years on the road

Nothing else. That's all you see. It's everywhere. There, I find a friend who has changed a lot during my African trip. When I left him in Diabet, he was poor like me, and now he has an almost new Land Rover.

He has a small, very flat briefcase. He opens it and shows me his treasures. Pieces of hashish from all over the world, of excellent quality, and several pills of different colors. He makes a chillum and gives it to me to light, which is a mark of politeness.

Ooh! That's a real slap in the face, I have to say I haven't smoked in a long time. Then he selects one of his little pills, puts it in my mouth without asking my opinion, and turns on his cassette player. "Number one quality acid," he tells me. He sticks a pair of super headphones on my ears. Pink Floyd on full blast! And he starts his car.

So we set off on the small mountain roads, at full speed. Of course, there's no protection, and we wouldn't survive in the event of an accident. The slopes are steep. We drive along the precipices at full speed. His acid is really strong. He climbs right up, and I start to freak out. This has never happened to me before. I'm completely terrified. I cling to the door handle. I'm in a complete panic. And I know this is going to last twelve hours! He stops. We cross fields of cannabis taller than me; he invites himself into some farmers' homes. At the back of the house, dozens of sheaves touch the ceiling. Sitting in a circle, he chats with them and tries to get him to give him a kilo to make a great hash.

I'm sitting on a mat, like everyone else. But I'm completely tense. I don't want to be here, or in this state. I clench my teeth until they feel like they're sinking into my jaws. Then we go see some other farmers. I try to tell him I'm freaking out, but he's not interested in me. I don't know if you can see that I'm completely panicked or not. From time to time, the Moroccan farmers give me a strange look.

Finally, after a few hours, I slowly come back down and calm down. I decide to stop taking LSD. Until then, it had been extremely positive, and now I'm discovering its negative side. It's a very powerful way to go deep into the positive and the very negative. Before, I only took my trips under the stars, in the countryside. Without the slightest noise, and it was perfect. And now, swallowed like that, without preparation, it's a disaster.

7 years on the road

Cannabis plants drying.

In fact, for the experience to go well, three conditions must be met. These three conditions are of equal importance and inseparable:
1 – have the mind ready,
2 – be in a favorable environment, without noise, without anything artificial, without other people not concerned by the experience,
3 – have good technique, a good product[1].
The product was supposed to be good, but my mood and the environment weren't. So, it was a failure, and very unpleasant.

It's high time to get down to business. I'm crossing Spain quickly and joining my parents on vacation on the Costa Brava, before returning with them to Brittany.

---

[1] I would discover this explanation about 50 years later in Rick Strassmann's book: "DMT, the Spirit Molecule." Exergue 2017.

7 years on the road

What surprises me most when I arrive in Saint-Brieuc is the bombings you see everywhere on the walls: "long live the joint", "the joint will win", "long live the French Joint"... I can't believe it. What's going on? When I left Saint-Brieuc I had never heard of joints, and now the demands are plastered all over the walls.

Well, actually, it has nothing to do with it. It's the Joint Français factory, which makes plumbing joints, that's on strike. All of Brittany is in solidarity.

I'm spending a few months at my parents' house. I'm working as an extra for a TV movie, in which I play the role of an American airman shot down by German flak and who reaches England, thanks to the Shelburn network. I'm writing a book about my last trip to Africa and I'm trying to get it published. It wasn't good and no one was interested. Finally, I'm leaving for India by plane with a return ticket that my parents gave me[1], even though I have no intention of coming back. I didn't expect it at all, I accept with pleasure, but I would have hitchhiked there anyway.

---

[1] While they are really far from being rich.

7 years on the road

7 years on the road

Namaste India

The plane taking me to Bombay—now Mumbai—isn't crowded. It's a small Kuwait Air Lines jet. It's not empty. It's one of the first charters, but it's nothing like ordinary charters, from what I understand. Behind me is a tall, thin man with very long hair. We switch seats so we're side by side. His name is Philippe. He goes to India twice a year and brings back things you can't find in Europe. No, not hashish or any other narcotic, but archaeological finds. Whether it's true or not, I don't care. I tell him what I want to do, and he says, "It's a baba trip." You can indeed call it that, even though I'm arriving by plane and have a return ticket, which I have no intention of using. I have no desire to return to Europe. I came to India to end my life living as a Sâdhu[1].

He tells me about Goa, the endless beach parties, the free acid. I think I'd better start there. Then I'll see. It must be pretty much the same atmosphere as Diabet, only much bigger and by the sea.

At the airport, I'm shocked. The hall is crowded with beggars of all kinds. It's much worse than all the misery I've seen so far, and I've seen a lot of it. Philippe explains to me that no one gives anything because if you do, you're immediately assaulted by the crowd who don't understand why you give to some people and not others. Later, I'll understand, but for now, no.

All in all, I have thirty-three dollars that I intend to spend as quickly as possible. I would have liked to distribute a little money to all these wretches—and that's an understatement—but it would have been a riot. I don't understand why they're all crammed into this filthy airport where no one gives them anything. It must be worse elsewhere, no doubt.

Outside, our taxi has to cross miles of shantytowns built on mud. It really stinks. The poor people we see are beggars who manage to stick their skeletal arms

---

[1] At 25 years old!

through our window and ask us for a little money. Just like at the airport, Philippe strongly advises me not to give anything, or we'll be invaded. The driver, who doesn't speak French, understands anyway and supports Philippe's argument in English.

It's the first shock. Such misery is terrifying. I remember the stories about bodies being picked up in the streets by municipal trucks. On a sidewalk, I see an old man lying on the ground, not moving. People are stepping over him. Is he dead?

But we go to an almost chic neighborhood and the poverty is less noticeable, despite the hundreds, even thousands, of small, meter-high shacks built on the sidewalks. People wash in the gutter. They have nothing, or almost nothing, because others, entire families, live outside with one or two saucepans and nothing else.

Families living on the streets.

Before getting off the plane, I noticed the antics of a gorgeous flight attendant. She kept busy stuffing the luggage in the net above the seats. It allowed her to show off her legs. Without a doubt, she was flirting with me. It didn't suit me at all, and I pretended I hadn't noticed. And then, Philippe got involved. He told me I had a ticket with the flight attendant. I told him I wasn't interested. He insisted. I continued to tell him I hadn't come to India for that. He kept quiet, and when we

7 years on the road

got off in Bombay, he outright invited the flight attendant to dinner that evening. Which she happily accepted, looking at me. All the way to the hotel Philippe knew, I grumbled. I told him there were going to be three of us. He tells me that she will come with a friend... That's indeed what will happen.

I won't tell you about the evening in the basement of the Taj Mahal Palace Hotel, but only that I messed everything up and Philippe must still be mad at me. And the hostesses too. But I didn't come to India for that!!!

I'm heading for Goa. I took a bus, since I still have about twenty-five dollars on me. I'm in a hurry to blow it and be truly poor. Like in all poor countries, the bus is packed. There are goats, sheep, chickens, and piles of bags of all kinds containing the most varied vegetables.

The weather is beautiful and warm. What strikes me most are the calendars in every shop we pass. They are portraits of Shiva, Ganesh, Parvati, Rama, Krishna, and tons of others I don't know. The champion of all categories is Shiva.

Shiva and Parvati (the benevolent and the mountain woman)

The expression "in India we live among the gods" is absolutely accurate. And there is music everywhere. Bhajans[1], including the famous " Raghupati Raghava Râja Ram" that we heard everywhere.

---

[1] Popular sacred songs.

7 years on the road

I'm happy, I'm beaming. It must show. Next to me, a little father dressed in orange smiles at me. He speaks a few words of English. He tells me that in Ahmedabad, there's an interesting temple to see. I'll see it later. For now, I'm heading due south, towards the heavenly beaches.

Many small white dry-stone walls connect the fields. Goa is a former Portuguese colony, and it shows. There are no temples, only Catholic churches. I have nothing against it, but I tell myself I'm on the wrong track again. However, I remember what my friends in Morocco and elsewhere told me. In Goa, people live under coconut trees. Some Westerners have rented houses not far from the beaches, which are very long. The one I'm going to, Anjuna Beach, is the third largest after Panaji Beach, which is pronounced Panjim. Panjim is where the post office and most of the shops are located.

It takes a while to get to Anjuna. I've always hated walking in the sand, and here I'm served, because the beaches are long. Once I arrive at Anjuna Beach, I take a look around. Hundreds of hippies live there. Many Americans. I don't really know the local customs, but I notice that people swim naked. It's logical, it's like that everywhere. Come on, hop, I put my things on the ground, I undress and I rush into the water. Wow, it's good! I'm quite sensitive to the cold, but I really appreciate it. I take a look under the coconut trees. There are people in circles smoking everywhere. I get out of the water, I gather my things and I head towards one of the circles. I sit down and take a drag on the chillum as he passes by. There, I'm not devastated. It's an average hash, the Black Bombay. It is mixed with opium, but the result is not great.

I look around and realize I'm the only one naked. No one makes any snide remarks, but I get dressed anyway. Apparently, you only get naked to swim.

I meet people I know from Morocco. The atmosphere is friendly. A few chillums are being passed around. It's Afghan. Not the devastating white chillum like the one in Bombay, at the Taj Mahal, but Mazar-i-Sharif, classic black chillum, one of the strongest in the world.

At the end of the beach, in a small shack, a group of people maintain a sound system blaring rock music. It's powered by a gasoline-powered generator. It's said to have been a gift from The Who.

7 years on the road

Cabin at Anjuna Beach 70s

I'm hanging around thinking I don't really like this kind of rock. They're far away Gene Vincent, Eddie Cochrane, Little Richard, and the other pioneers. And then, the guys turn it up too loud. The sound thumps. It's unnecessary aggression.

The sun is about to set. As I'm wondering where I'm going to settle down, I hear someone shouting: "Acid, Acid!!!!" A big, bearded American man, dressed in white, is brandishing a laboratory jar three-quarters full of a colorless liquid and a glass pipette. It's clear, he just made it in Anjuna Beach. An area that has no electricity! It must be simple to make. One of the guys I know tells me it's pure Acid and that it's free. I had decided not to take any more. Here, the conditions are different. I'm in India, I'm the one who decides and will lead my trip.
I get in line, and when it's my turn, I only take three drops. The one before me took seven.

I watch the sunset. It's a sight worth the trip. Magnificent. But I quickly realize that all the beaches are in total darkness and the only lit area is the sandy "dance floor" right next to the sound system. I don't know where to go.

On the one hand, the music is too loud and I have no desire to dance; on the other, it's night and I don't know the place. I could sit back and look at the stars, but I

7 years on the road

can't. At the same time, I want to blend in with the group in the light. These two desires are incompatible. So I spend the night like an idiot, on the edge of the light, moving forward and back depending on the loudness of the music. From time to time, I see a group pass by and push away a dancer who is clearly more scared than me. They ask if anyone has a Mandrax—a powerful Indian sleeping pill, the only way to effectively end one's journey.

The next day, I sleep through the day and stay away from the music. I'm slumped in a hut made by poor French people who cough up their lungs with every chillum. They're nice, but anyway, I've decided to leave for Varanasi—Banares—the next day.

I return to Panjim, passing Indian families strolling along the beaches. The fathers sneakily glance at each other. The wives and children look rather bored. The naked young hippies jumping in the waves are a sight worth seeing.

Arriving in Panjim, I buy two colored sheets: one yellow and one light orange. I change in front of everyone, gather my jeans and shirt in my rolled-up blanket. In a small woolen satchel, I have my I Ching. I also have a small cloth bag under my left shoulder where I have my passport and all my smoking accessories. But I still have some money. Because twenty-five dollars is a lot of rupees. I'm disappointed, because I thought I could help the broke in Goa, but no one was interested. So I take the bus back to Bombay to blow everything and then I'll hitchhike to Banares.

Near the station, I meet people I met in Morocco. They show me the place of Bombay where the hippies and junkies hang out. There's a hotel packed with long-haired, bearded men who smoke like African trucks. A dozen professional gurus, dressed in clean, ironed orange sheets, are laying siege to the hotel, trying to find a disciple, if possible American and not too poor.

Their first attack is "From witch country do you belong?" With a laugh-out-loud accent. They're all dressed in orange, with long hair, but not too long. And a small, trimmed beard. They smell so much like a scam that I don't bother to answer them.

7 years on the road

We're drinking chai on a terrace near the hotel. A beautiful Parisian woman is there. She's addicted to opium. She smokes it. To make a living, she acts as an extra in Bollywood films. She's happy like that and has no desire to return to Paris.

My friends tell her I've just arrived and would like to smoke at least a pipe. They figured that out on their own; I didn't ask. We first go to a restaurant where they eat well and can drink wine. I'll pay.

I had a different idea of opium dens. This one is super basic. No fabric, no cushions. Nothing at all. Just cement and a newspaper for a bed, whose pages, placed end to end, are about two meters long. A wooden cube serves as a pillow. We are in a room of a building under construction. The Indians who run the smokehouse are skeletal. Several people are waiting their turn.

When it's my turn, I lie down on the newspaper, grumbling to myself. The guy takes care of the pipe, prepares the opium, and tells me when I can start. At first, nothing. I don't feel anything, as is often the case with new hashish smokers, so I say nothing. And then all of a sudden, the cement and wood become very comfortable. I've never had such a nice bed. The guy signals me to get up when the pellet is finished, to make room for the others. No problem, I'm happy to share. I get up and then I rush outside and vomit my meal. Afterward, I feel much better. All opium derivatives cause this in novices. Perhaps it's a signal from the body to warn of the product's dangers? In any case, the mixture with red wine doesn't go well at all.

The effect gives a feeling of well-being. I feel confident, I'm completely right, I'm a really good guy. Of course, it's completely artificial, but I understand those who become addicted to it. And I pity them because once they're hooked, the lack becomes unbearable, both mentally and physically.

7 years on the road

Next to the Taj Mahal

I left Bombay on foot. This time, I don't have a cent left. I feel free and in a great mood. I head towards Ahmedabad. I go to see the famous temple the old man told me about. Hitchhiking works quite well. It's mostly trucks that pick me up. What surprises me is the incredible population that travels on both sides of the road on foot, by bicycle, in camel-drawn carts. I come across my first elephant, carrying a mattress on its shoulders on which an Indian man, lying on his side, is peacefully daydreaming.

What I love about Indians is the way they greet each other. With clasped hands, we respect each other. It might not seem like much, but in reality, it changes everything. Despite caste and despite humankind's need to harm, there reigns a great peace that can almost be touched. But I'm talking about the countryside. Anyone who only visits big cities only sees one aspect of India. And vice versa.

7 years on the road

The truck stops near a diner lined with calendars in praise of Shankar—one of the 108 names of Shiva. The driver, who's super friendly but hasn't opened his mouth since I climbed into the cab, gets out to go get a bite to eat. Since I don't have a rupee left, I stay in the truck. The restaurant owner exchanges a few words with the driver while looking at me. He signals for me to join him. I let him know I have no money. He explains to me in Hindi with a few words of English that I can eat whatever I want. I thank him. He refuses the thanks, explaining that it is God who gives to God and makes a grand gesture to make me understand that the universe and its contents are God, or even more. "Bhagavan," he says. So everything is God. I am deeply touched by it. I think about that moment almost every day, even now.

Finally, I arrive in Ahmedabad. It's a medium-sized city by Indian standards. That is to say, you can walk through it without being crushed by the crowd. I find the temple that brought me here. It's ugly. It's a modern concrete building. I could almost have walked past it without noticing it. I go in. Inside, it's the complete opposite of the outside. Lots of colors, predominantly red, orange, and yellow. Brass instruments of all kinds: cymbals, trays, gongs... The priests are all fat and healthy. They are Brahmins. In front of them are piles of flowers, powders of all colors, rose petals, water with a small scoop to pour into the hands... I am dazzled by the atmosphere. The faithful go around the priests and each time give a few paesas, which are the cents of rupees.

7 years on the road

One of the Brahmins beckons me over. He draws a red line between my eyes. I explain that I have no money for the offering. He shows me a spot next to him and motions for me to sit down. I take out my I Ching and do a lot of random se lections. The Brahmin smiles silently, but I'm not at all sure he knows what this is about. Then I'm invited to eat with them. A plate of dhal[1] with rice. Eat with your hands. What am I saying? With your hand! The right hand, the other is used to wash your bottom. They don't use paper in poor countries.

I thank them and go for a walk around the city. I forgot that Hindu rules are not the same as Muslim ones. I think I'm invited to stay and sleep in the temple. This is a mistake. In India, there are many temples, some of which are designed to ac commodate travelers. This one isn't one of them. But I don't know that yet.

I pass by a neighborhood, a kind of slum without the glaring poverty of those in Bombay. I meet a young guy dressed halfway in European style. He speaks a few words of English. We chat a little and I suggest we smoke a chillum. He accepts. However, I sense that he is not a regular smoker. Nevertheless, I make one and it makes us extremely cheerful. We go to the temple to show him where my place is. It is empty, except for a Brahmin who is busy in his corner. And we always come out very cheerful. A little later, he goes home, and I return to the temple. And, in the place I occupied, I find my things neatly arranged. And not a priest around. That's clear. I am being thrown out. I take my things and continue on my way. As I walk, I wonder what is the reason for this expulsion. Was it because I was intruding or because I had let an untouchable in? Or both? Or because I was too gay? More than forty years later, I still ask myself this question. But it still doesn't keep me awake at night.

On the way to Udaipur. Well, the destination is Banares, Varanasi in Hindi and other languages, probably including Sanskrit, but I'm in no hurry and I'm taking my time. Rajasthan is a magnificent country. A little dry, but beautiful. Even more than that, we're entering a new dimension. Udaipur is, unlike other Indian cities, not too crowded, but very hot and noisy. In Goa, the sacred cows weren't very respected by the Catholics, who would give them a little nudge on the nose when they tried to graze on a merchant's stall. Here, it's different. There's one blocking the main intersection. The Indians are trying to get it to move by offer-

---

[1]Lentils.

ing it vegetables. It won't listen. The truck and car drivers are furious, but no one touches it.

I chat with a lot of people I meet. Not many of them speak English. I can see that some of them wonder why a Westerner would give up everything to be half-Sâdhu. Abandon a rich country where people earn a lot of money, drive Mercedes, and where women are blonde and sexually liberated. They don't ask the question, but I sense they're thinking it.

Holy cow that's being curious.

There aren't many cars, only Tatas, but there are plenty of beautifully decorated trucks. Hitchhiking works well, but I want to try the train. I've been told that Sâdhus don't pay. I'll take my chance just in case.

Oh, what a crowd! The trains are jammed. They remind me of the buses in Cairo, only worse. I board third class. There's a baba standing at the back of the carriage I'm boarding. The conductor passes by and asks for my ticket. I tell him I don't have one. He insists. The Sâdhu follows this silently, a small smile on his lips. The conductor, a little lost, finally gives in and turns to him. What has he done there! He gets a hearty scolding, with rare virulence. You don't ask a saint if he has his ticket!

Indian trains almost empty.

The inspector doesn't insist and continues his inspection. I discover one thing: A Sâdhu is capable of violence, at least verbally, if we consider him an ordinary man. He is a man who renounces everything, possesses nothing. Dressed in a sheet—a longi—but sometimes naked, covered in ashes, he is not a simple person. Some of them are "warriors," sometimes carrying a saber or a trident, like Shiva. It's purely symbolic, of course; there is nothing more peaceful than a Sâdhu. But he mustn't be bothered. Which, in principle, no one does.

He owns nothing. The Sâdhu is a renunciant. A "sanyasin." He renounces everything: his name, his caste, his family, to own anything, apart from what he can carry: his lota, a small tin pot that serves for everything, and his chillum. In Europe he would be considered a tramp and a drug addict, here he is venerated and respected. A little feared too. He is supposed to be endowed with extraordinary powers.

I've seen some who set goals, like looking the sun straight in the eye, but never anyone aggressive. The ones I know or meet are renunciants who go on pilgrimages to holy places. They are very peaceful, owning almost nothing, neither trident nor copper lota.

Times are changing!!!

The baba gives me a small, knowing smile. He's covered in ashes with a large red line down the middle of his forehead. His hair is rolled in the ash like dreadlocks. A shaggy beard falls onto his stomach. But he doesn't engage in conversation. Sadhus aren't talkative, and even less curious.

After long, arduous hours in this overcrowded train, we arrive in Ajmer. I get off there, the Sâdhu continues.

I'm pleasantly crossing Ajmer. It's a city significantly smaller than Udaipur and, of course, Bombay. I'm leisurely following a street heading towards Jaipur, the Pink City, when I'm struck by a sight that's completely incongruous in India. A beef carcass is hanging outside a butcher's shop. A small group of Indians are chatting in front of it. One of them speaks to me in English. I put down my things and join in the conversation. They're friendly and curious. I tell them how much I think of India. And then, after a while of chatting, I have to pee. I glance around and head towards the first wall I see. Before I can release a drop, I hear the whole group shouting. I lower my longi and turn around. They shout at me, "This is the mosque." Good God, I was about to pee on a mosque! I had forgotten that there were quite a few Muslims in India, although the beef carcass should have immediately indicated that.

I arrive in Jaipur. It's a bigger city than Udaipur. It's the city of the Jains. A very ancient religion (about 2,600 years old) that venerates life in all its forms. Killing any animal whatsoever is out of the question. The priests wear a white mask over their mouths to prevent them from swallowing an insect. A worshipper sweeps in front of their feet so they don't crush a single ant, using a strange broom with a short handle and long white bristles. Their Sâdhus are completely naked and completely beardless.

Water Palace, Jaipur

I chat with a lot of people. They're curious and very nice. They don't all speak English, but there's always one who can and acts as an interpreter for his friends. The same questions often come up: why leave a rich country to come and live in poverty? I explain to them that rich countries are only rich from a material point of view and that they are lucky to live in a country rich in spirituality, and that poverty is only physical poverty.

7 years on the road

They don't believe me at all, or they think I'm crazy. They might be right. Who knows? But you can still feel that they're very proud of their country and their culture.

And I'm back on the road to Varanasi. I'm not taking the shortest route. I'm in no hurry. Everyone's telling me to go to Agra to see the Taj Mahal. So, I'm going. I don't really care, but if they insist that I go, it's probably because I'm going to meet someone there.

The Taj and its lake

Agra's reputation is, of course, due to the mausoleum where the favorite wife of one of the Muslim Mughal emperors has been buried for some time after the failed delivery of her 14th child. But it's also the Red Fort, which you can't miss when visiting the wonder of the world. It seems to be occupied by a symbolic regiment. This is probably more to maintain the fort than anything else. But I could be wrong.

Arriving at the Taj Mahal, the truck stops. I thank the driver by clasping my hands. He nods in agreement. Like all drivers, he's not talkative. He understands very little English. That suits me just fine.

7 years on the road

I'm lucky, admission is free. It's crowded. But it's not a problem, as visitors wander through the parks and gardens. It must be said that with the lakes, we have a very beautiful, if somewhat neglected, setting. Lots of families. Muslims and Hindus. It must be mealtime, because the mothers are bringing out their picnics on the yellow lawns.

I take the opportunity to go inside. Nothing but white marble and inlaid semi-precious stones. The sculptors seem more gifted than those who made our European churches and calvaries at the same time. It's a true masterpiece. But I feel something. Like tangible vibrations. Do the other visitors feel them? Good question. They all seem serious, whether Hindu or Muslim, and deeply moved. After the visit, I sit on a lawn next to a body of water. I appreciate the moment.

I see a hairy backpacker approaching. He heads straight for me. He's English. We don't talk much. I take out a piece of Charas[1] and prepare a chillum. I didn't make it too strong, but it works.

He asks me where the temple is where we can sleep. I don't know. But, since there are temples everywhere in India, there must be one around here.

A young Indian man, no older than 30, at first glance dressed in new orange sheets and with very long, neatly combed hair, approaches us. He speaks perfect English. He shaves. He doesn't have a single hair out of place.

Curious. He's the one guarding the temple we're talking about. He invites us and shows us the way. It's located right next to the sultana's tomb, down below, along the Yamuna River.

Moreover, another detail jumps out at me late in the afternoon: The second part of the temple is used by disciples who are very busy. Logically, it's the travelers' place to occupy the cement where they do their exercises. And, still logically, it should be their place to frequent Sri Khan Baba.

In any case, they are impressive. They are Indians who have finished their work. They are bodybuilding with whatever means they have. Hanging from a cement gantry, doing push-ups and other exercises I didn't know. When they are finished,

---
[1]Hashish in Hindi.

they clean themselves noisily with loud buckets of water drawn from the Yamuna. Then, one of them takes out a handful of ganja. He grinds it into a pulp, watering it abundantly, using a cylindrical stone on another flat stone. This lasts for a while, then he takes a cup, like an Army tin mug, carefully mixes the mushy grass and the water. Then, they stand in a circle and pass the mug around. I am part of the circle, I take a small sip.

Behind the Taj Mahal

This is the famous bhang. In its raw state! Then they take out the cigarette packs and decks of cards, and they play as if nothing happened. This is my first bhang, it won't be the last. It's particularly strong.

In our courtyard, among the Westerners, there are two beautiful American women traveling together. I find that Sri Khan Baba is very interested in them. They don't seem to appreciate it. He is roughly put back in his place and a slight unease reigns.

7 years on the road

Traditional preparation of Bhang

I don't appreciate this atmosphere at all and decide to hit the road again for Banares. It's not impossible that I'll return to Agra. This little temple is still very pleasant and well-shaded. And Sri Khan Baba is very kind, when he doesn't have what I'm thinking instead of a brain. The conversation with him is pleasant, even if he probably knows the Beatles' discography better than the Vedas.

The only slight inconvenience is the corpses of those who cannot afford to be cremated. They are thrown as is into the Yamuna. It is considered sacred. Less so than the Ganges, but it is rather beneficial. The bodies remain near the temple for a while between two waters in the water of the Yamuna. After a few days, they are carried away by the gentle current and go a little further. They remain there until they wash up on the bank and are eaten by stray dogs. It makes more than one person shudder.

7 years on the road

Varanasi, at last!

The truck drops me off at the entrance to Banares—Varanasi—where it parks next to dozens of others, all super-decorated with peacocks, Hindu gods, swastikas, and so on. I ask a guy passing by the area for directions to the Ganges and dive into the crowd. I've never seen such a multitude attacking from all directions: bicycles, rickshaws, cars, dromedaries, elephants, carts, and pedestrians, not to mention the corpses on stretchers held at arm's length by a few men rushing toward the Shamshan Ghat where people have been cremating without a single stop for 2,300 years.

The closer I get to the Ganges, the more Sâdhus I see, real and fake. These Sâdhus are dressed in orange and beg, among them there are lepers and various types of disabled people. The real Sâdhu does not beg. He accepts donations and if he is not given anything, well, he simply does not eat. A little further on, there are some money changers. They transform the rupee into 99 paesas. The pilgrims have their hands full and can give a little to each beggar. In the final stretch before the Dashashvamedha Ghat, the beggars sit on both sides of the alley,

There is something for everyone, not much, but for everyone.

in which only pedestrians circulate, behind a small container. The pilgrims leave each person a few paesas or a pinch of rice.

And here is the Ganges! It's an immense river. The water is clear and shows no visible signs of pollution. The ghat is, in fact, a very wide staircase. There are lots of people sitting, and a huge crowd of very silent pilgrims. I appreciate the calm that reigns. There is no more noise. The pilgrims are going to perform their ablutions, and even to drink the water of the sacred river. I do the same, without knowing the gestures and mantras to say, but I bathe and then I go back up to the ghat.

I sit quietly. I'm tired from my journey through Varanasi. It's either madness or recklessness. And yet, at that time, India had only 400 million inhabitants. Now, there are nearly a billion and a half. I wonder how they manage to get around. In any case, this crossing, on foot of course, was particularly difficult. I was even hit by a bicycle brake lever.

A group of Sâdhus is a few meters away from me. They are sitting in a circle around a fire. The hearth is made of sacred cow dung diluted in water and dried. It's completely white, like cement. The babas are almost naked and covered in ash. They are silent and gaze calmly at the hearth.

7 years on the road

The one who appears to be the guardian of the fire, whom I call "the main baba," gives me a sign I had already noticed when I arrived at the ghat. He rubs his right thumb in his left hand. This is the gesture of someone who mixes charas with tobacco to prepare a chillum. I signal to him that I have nothing. He lets me know that it doesn't matter and invites me to join them.

For me, it's an honor. It goes straight to my heart. I sit with them. I don't have to take off my shoes since I walk barefoot. I sit cross-legged like them, and I don't ask any questions, just like them. I notice that the fire is fueled by wood from the Shamshan Ghat that was used for cremation. The ash produced becomes even more sacred.

No one asks me anything, but I decide to find something to smoke from the passing Westerners. As soon as I see one with long hair and a backpack, I ask him if he has any hash—they are almost all English-speaking. I explain to them that I'm with a group of babas who would like to smoke a little. Most of the time, they agree. They take off their shoes before sitting down; I'm uncompromising. The Westerners greet the sâdhus, give them a piece of hash, or directly prepare a chillum. The nicest ones leave a piece, for me or for the main baba. Needless to say, this gift is immediately consumed, in several installments if necessary.

I wonder how I'm going to manage to eat. No one talks about it, but I'm starting to get hungry. I see most of the beggars set up shop on either side of the alley leading to the ghat. So I go there too. A trunk-man dressed in orange has just been dropped off by another guy right in front of me. He's good-looking, and if he had arms and legs, he should have been a hit with the ladies.

A group approaches, preceded by a uniformed cop, club in hand. An Indian distributes chapatis—unleavened bread—to each beggar. Two of his colleagues carry an enormous cauldron full of dhal, well-prepared lentils. I eat like this for a few days. And then I see that the Sâdhus aren't moving, and that the guys doing the distribution are going to serve them at their places around the fire.

So I decide to stay with the group for the next few times. In the evening, they come to our circle, we hand them our lotas—small metal boxes that are used for everything—like milk jugs for the simplest—and they fill them.

We feast in silence. You don't eat every day as a traveling ascetic. So we appreciate it slowly. This distribution of food is called prasad. These are Indians with income who donate funds to one or more temples to feed the poor, just to feel good about their conscience and, if possible, score points for the next reincarnation.

Night falls, and the spectacle is truly beautiful. The pilgrims place a small candle in a tree leaf. They place them all on the water at the same time at nightfall. It creates a whole luminous flotilla descending the Ganges.

One of the temples bordering the ghat is packed. Chants rise up, accompanied by the sound of conch shell cymbals and bells, against a backdrop of tablas. It's beautiful. Especially from the outside, because they're still crammed into the temple.

My fellow Babas sometimes sing, accompanied by the clanging of their tong-shaped pokers, some of which carry small cymbals. They don't sing temple songs, but rather what are called bhajans, that is, sung mantras.

Every now and then, a pilgrim comes to see the chief baba, touches his feet, and asks him something. The other answers him in a few words and draws a line of ash between his eyes. The pilgrim leaves him a few paesas before leaving. I have no idea what it is, but I suppose it is advice or a blessing.

At times, they all sit cross-legged. I wonder if they're meditating or reciting mantras to themselves. To be honest, I don't know what meditation is. I imagine it's a kind of introspection. So I do the same, reflecting on everything I discover. Pretty quickly, I understand that the Sâdhu doesn't meditate, doesn't say mantras, or anything like that. He doesn't have to, since he's a Sâdhu. But if he wants to, he can.

7 years on the road

One day I realize I have no idea what month I'm in. I could have been in Banares for three weeks or three months, I have no idea.
Every day, I go hunting for Charas. All the long-haired, bearded Westerners with backpacks all have a little. It works very well. They are very proud to be invited by Sâdhus.

Bom Shankar!

The group of babas changes from time to time; some leave, others arrive. They simply greet and sit down. No one asks them anything.

I've just pulled the chillum. I'm passing it to my neighbor, who's much older than the others, when I hear a scream. There's a fight going on at the top of the ghat, the likes of which you only see in India. The object of the dispute is an old green blanket. The protagonists are: on one side, a sacred cow, and on the other, the baba who owns the said blanket. She's eating it. He doesn't agree and pulls his own way. Finally, the blanket tears in two and everyone gets their share. It must be said that grass doesn't grow on the ghats, and the sacred cows don't have much to eat. The baba is angry and leaves, not at all happy, with his half-blanket.

7 years on the road

We only eat in the evening. We feast on prasad. It often alternates. One day rice, the next day chapatis, all with dhal[1]. It's very good. It's what we all look forward to every evening. But, for once, there's a real crush. The fake sâdhus pounce on the one distributing the chapatis. The big cop hits it with his club, not too hard, but enough. Finally, the one who distribute heads towards our group with a pile of chapatis. It's Versailles tonight! I rejoice, racked with hunger. But the guy is so jostled that he puts his foot with his shoe in the circle formed by the Sâdhus. Then the main baba takes on a furious look, shows him his foot and signals him to leave. He refuses the prasad.

Tough, tough! We remain hungry. It's hard to give up everything. But Sâdhus are like that. We owe them respect.

I notice that there are a lot of tourists who want to take their pictures. They refuse vigorously, even very vigorously. So the smart tourists rent a canoe, park in front of the ghat, and take pictures of everyone.

There are a few shops and two or three chai shops not far from the ghats, at the top of the alley. One of them serves lassis—liquid yogurt—straight or bhang-lassis, for ten paesas extra. From time to time, I go there to drink a bhang-lassi. It's treacherous because it takes about twenty minutes for it to work, and then: whoop! It hits! With this, you don't need a chillum.

Bhang balls: 0.10 rupees each.

Across from the chai shop, there's a market stall like the kind we'd like to see more of. Officially, it sells umbrellas. There are four of them, hanging from a metal bar in a corner of the stall. In the middle, there's a huge burlap sack, at least

---

[1]Lentils.

two hundred liters, full of cannabis. A large scale hangs in the middle of the place. He sells by the kilo or pound using a grain scoop. In the front display, on a shelf, ready-made bhang balls, different types of charas, small opium balls—the kind you swallow—chillums, and other smoking paraphernalia await customers. The bhang balls and opium balls are worth ten paesas. Business is good for the owner; he's selling non-stop.

he scales have changed

One day, while out hunting for Charas, I find the crowd as noisy as I've ever heard it. The kids, wearing large white shirts over their clothes, have bicycle pumps in their hands and are squirting paint at everyone. I don't like it at all. I have the impression that the whole town is drunk on alcohol —which is forbidden in the state of Uttar Pradesh. I go back to the babas and show them my displeasure. They signal me not to worry. They all say "Holi." I don't understand. I'll only find out many years later. It's a religious festival called Holi, during which everyone throws color at each other, by any means necessary. Practically all Hindus drink bhang that day. Men and especially women. I still notice that the kids aren't trying to color the Sâdhus. Two of the kids follow me to the circle where I'm sitting. But they don't dare continue.

7 years on the road

Another day, two plainclothes cops came up to me, sitting with my renouncers. They asked to see my passport. I still had it. They looked at the visa and left me alone. The babas didn't intervene. I flinched a little. Later, I realized that this was happening outside their own world. The cops didn't ask them anything, and they didn't concern themselves with the society they had renounced. Whereas I, with my passport and my return ticket, hadn't renounced anything.

It's still an indication, my visa is still valid, so I've been in India for less than three months.
This check worries me and I feel it's time for me to leave, because holy city or not, Varanasi is above all a city. I've heard about the sources of the Ganges and the tranquility of the place. So, one morning, I pack up my things. I greet the babas and I leave. Direction Hardwar. One of the holiest cities in India.

7 years on the road

7 years on the road

Hardwar, Rishikesh.

On my way to the foothills of the Himalayas. First stop: Hardwar[1]. I take the train without a ticket. The conductor arrives, and I tell him I don't have a ticket. He absolutely wants me to pay. I don't care and I persist. He threatens to call the train police. I get off at the next stop. I continue hitchhiking and on foot. I take the opportunity to get my thoughts in order. I'm not Indian. I'm a Westerner, like so many others in Goa, Bombay, or Delhi. A guy who will never be fully integrated into Indian life.

The road to Hardwar is long. I meet Westerners from time to time. Only in small towns. I flee the cities where I can no longer stand the noise and crowds. We smoke a lot and exchange anecdotes. They generally go to Varanasi and come from Rishikesh. They tell me that in Hardwar there is a large gathering of sâdhus permanently. It is not the Kumbha mela, the great festival that takes place every twelve years[2], from what I understand, where hundreds of thousands of sâdhus meet – they are estimated to be several million in total. It is the only opportunity to see those who live only in the forests or in the caves of the Himalayas. But you have to wait a few years.

Finally, I arrive in Hardwar. It's a pretty little town on the banks of the Ganges, where the houses are brightly colored.

You can't miss the sâdhus; there are thousands of them gathered in a large park along the Ganges, which is much narrower than in Banares. There don't seem to be any fake sâdhus. Those who are there are, for the most part, naga babas cov-

---

[1] This city is now called Haridwar, dedicated to Vishnu, but everyone says Hardwar, dedicated to Shiva.
[2] It takes place every 12 years in Allahabad, and every 4 years in three other cities including Hardwar.

ered in ash. Some, not the most numerous, don't smoke and are more likely disciples of Vishnu. I find myself adopted by a small group of Shiva followers. They are more talkative but don't speak English. They aren't curious and make themselves understood by gestures. I should learn Hindi. We all go swimming in the Ganges. It's freezing.

A "modern" Indian, that is, one who is dressed like a Westerner, with short hair and no beard, approaches me and, in the blink of an eye, balances on his head. It's an asana, a yoga posture, called shirshasana. He stays in this posture for a good ten minutes. Then he speaks to me in perfect English. He invites me to come with him to beg. I would only have to sit in the lotus position and he would balance on his head. If there were only one yoga posture, they say it would be shishasana. The blood rushes to the head and it's excellent for all sorts of things. But maybe not all day long! This extremely friendly guy spends at least half his time in this position. It makes him very happy. Exuberant, he's overflowing with happiness. We sit down at the exit of a department store and stay for about half an hour. The recipe is quite good. But anyway, I'll stop. I didn't come here to beg. And holding the lotus pose becomes difficult. He, on the other hand, is very expansive. He has a very pervasive happiness.

I return to my group of babas after sharing the recipe with him. I buy a large piece of hashish from an "umbrella" store.
My yogi, who only smokes English cigarettes, sits on his head next to us while we prepare a chillum. The babas smile.

I observe one who spends his day staring at the sun. "It is by becoming blind that he will achieve enlightenment," I say to myself, smiling.

Another day, a sâdhu came to see me. He explained that it would be nice to come with him to smoke a sâdhvi, whom he called Mata-ji. A female sâdhu. I didn't know such a thing existed.
She lives in a sort of cave, deep in the park, dug into a large grove. It's hard to see her. Before entering, the sâdhu signals to me not to shout "Bom Shankar!" when lighting the chillum.
She has transformed her little plant cave into a small temple. We greet each other in silence, simply joining hands. I prepare the chillum. Instinctively, I shout "Bom..." and then I remember that I shouldn't have done it. She doesn't say any

7 years on the road

thing. The sâdhu must be thinking that Westerners are what they are, that is, tourists in longi. He just gives me the evil eye. But we smoke our chillum quietly. I leave them a good piece before leaving.

And then a few days later, I set off for Rishikesh. I'm going on foot; it's twenty-four kilometers away. The air is much fresher than in Varanasi. My spirits are better than when I left Banares. I'm still a little disturbed by this police check. But I love walking in the countryside. Not just any countryside. The one that goes up the Ganges. I'm not following the main road, but a small path.

And there, at a bend in the path, I find a French-speaking guy chatting with a baba sitting cross-legged, his elbow resting on a portable armrest, specially designed to only lean on it while sitting cross-legged. They both welcome me very cordially.

The old reflexes return. I take out the chillum and a piece of hashish. The three of us take a drag. After a while, the French-speaker tells me that the baba was buried alive for a week. I admire him. I know there are sâdhus who perform feats of this kind. Some roll around for months to go on a pilgrimage, others lift rocks with their genitals. Still others remain their entire lives with one arm in the air or standing on one foot.

This one looks about twenty-five. But one hair in his beard is completely white. Just one. He speaks a little English. He tells me he's thirty-five.
They're going to Rishikesh, so we team up. Alain, the French speaker, tells me he's going to spend some time in the caves along the Ganges. I'm tempted. I'll go with him.

Rishikesh! Here we are. The Ganges is really narrow compared to Banares. You still have to cross it by boat. Rishikesh isn't yet the spiritual supermarket it's become. It's a prosperous little town. It lives off its supplies to the ashrams. There are some everywhere, all around. A helicopter crosses the sky as we leave a shop. It's that of the Maharishi Mahesh Yogi, the Beatles' guru. He's picking up clients at the nearest airport.

We ask a swami dressed all in orange, where to go to reach the caves. He explains it to us in very understandable English. We thank him and as we leave, he adds that if we want to buy Charas we can contact him. That blows me away coming from a swami!

We cross the Ganges in a curious boat with a glass bottom. This allows us to see enormous fish. Of course, they are sacred; no one would think of bringing a fishing rod.

There are several caves, some of which are occupied, either by Westerners, sâdhus, or a solitary baba meditating. We find one that is clean and already has a dhuni—sacred fire. We make ourselves a chillum. It's good! As good neighbors, we invite the babas near us. They are happy to join us in the cave. The chillums are turned for our greatest pleasure. But the language barrier still bothers me. We can see that they like us, and that we could talk a little. We understand each other through gestures and interposed words or phrases: Bom Shankar, pani—water; atcha—yes; chapatis; flatbread—alou gobi—cauliflower and potatoes... It's still limited. But since no one is curious, it's fine like that.

Rishikesh in the 70s, there was no bridge yet.

7 years on the road

In the evening, everyone comes to eat rice and dhal, prepared by one of the Westerners, under the suspicious eye of one of the babas. Don't forget the spices! And the hotter it is, the better it is. Everyone takes out their hash and we make comparisons. Pakistani is worthless, it makes the sâdhus laugh. I think that for them, anything from Pakistan is worthless anyway.

An Englishman pulls out a strange piece. It's black on top and green on the inside. He explains that it's produced near Chitral in Pakistan. It's far north, in the Himalayas. And the chillums are still spinning. I notice for the first time, after quite a bit of practice, that they always spin clockwise.

Ooh! What a slap! The babas don't criticize anymore. Nobody can talk anymore, anyway. After a while, Alain says he's stronger than fresh Manali.

Everyone knows that Manali hashish, or Charas by its Indian name, is one of the best on the planet. But it has one major drawback: it must be smoked fresh. It doesn't keep very well.

Alain tells us about Manali, the paradise of cannabis. It's not a sacred place but a winter sports resort where wealthy families come to spend some time, just for a change of scenery. So why is it a paradise? Well, because cannabis grows everywhere. Like dandelions in our climate. Simply stroke the plant gently between the palms of your hand, gently moving up towards the top of the plant. Then all that's left is to scrape your hands together, one against the other, when they are nice and black. The resin clumps into small rolls, which you then have to assemble. Indeed, it's quite tempting.

After a few days, I leave Rishikesh with Alain. I don't really like the ashram atmosphere around me, even though I haven't been to see a single one. I suspect I'll find a swami, speaking English, who will ask me "from witch country do you be long?" with an Indian accent. The stay must not be free and, theoretically, you can't smoke in those areas. Everything is based on meditation which leads to a higher level of consciousness. The same one you get after a good chillum, smoked in a state of spiritual research, according to what an Indian teacher explained to me. This is what a few babas have already made me understand. They passed this stage long ago. Besides, when you ask an Indian why sâdhus smoke Charas, he replies: "It helps them meditate."

7 years on the road

It doesn't take long for me to see mountains getting higher and higher. I'm not very warm, with my longi and the other one on my back. But that's the life of—almost—renouncers. The valley leading to Manali is very narrow. We're definitely in the Himalayas, there's no doubt about it. It's not Everest, but it's high. My truck stops at Kullu. It's the last reasonably large town before Manali. No temple in sight. It's getting late. I ask a passerby if he knows the temple where we can sleep. He gives me directions, very kindly.

Well, it's not a super-temple like the ones we know in South India. It's like the one in Agra and many others, that is to say, on one side the residence of the guardian baba, who receives his "disciples" in his garden during the day, and on the other side a cement space around a hearth, with just a roof held up by cement posts, and two walls. And in front of the temple, behind the flowerbeds, the river flows peacefully. This river is mentioned in the Rig Veda under its ancient name: the Vipasha.

I sit down in front of the hearth, the dhuni. The baba comes to see me. He's not an ordinary baba, that's obvious. He must be around 50 years old and wears a turban. He's very happy to see me. He takes out his chillum and squats on his heels. The chillum turns, I make another one with my piece of hashish. And the baba explains to me, as best he can, that he's a chapati specialist and would be particularly happy to show me how to make them. I explain to him that I'm going to Manali, but that I'll be back.

Manali

Indeed, in Manali, we leave the world of spirituality behind. Not a single baba, but we meet Tibetan refugees. Many monks in full dress, but sometimes wearing watches, which leaves me a little perplexed. In the crowd of Westerners, I recognize a few hippies I saw in Goa.

Manali: city center

It's a large village where wealthy Indians come to ski. Manali is divided into two parts: the village, with the shops, and the houses rented to Westerners by the peasants who suddenly get rich. This area is of no interest, except to shelter us from the cold. We're still at 1,826 meters. My two pieces of cotton are no longer enough. I take my jeans and sweater out of my blanket.

These are the kinds of houses that Westerners lived in.

When I was told that cannabis grew everywhere, it was true. There are some on every ditch and in the middle of the main "square," some three-meter-high. There are several in front of the post office and all the way to the police station entrance.

I meet a few guys I knew in Morocco, and it gives me great pleasure. Among them, there's one who's manipulating the dates on visas. I take the opportunity to see how long it's been since I arrived. It's been well past three months. Good God, I wonder where I could have stayed so long. Banares, yes, of course, Hardwar and Rishikesh, probably longer than I thought. During that time, I've lived outside of time. One dimension less. It's weird.

My friend changes my visa date. He does it really well, you can't see anything.

7 years on the road

I spend a few days gently rubbing all the cannabis plants I find, and I scratch my hands over a scarf. The Charas is good. But since I'm not the first to do it, the re sult isn't great. Some plants, rubbed every day by Westerners who come "down town," are pathetic. You have to go a little further than Manali to find untouched "gold mines." Not far, they're everywhere.

When you're in the village, you have to go back up in the evening if you want to be a little warm, and that's a different story. The path that climbs to the houses is almost vertical. Some use it without any problems, and others, too stoned to climb it, sit in a small meadow opposite and smoke a few chillums to give them selves courage. As a result, the more you smoke, the less strength you have. So I go there in several stages.

One evening, in one of the houses I'm staying at, I look at my return plane ticket. (Well done, the renouncer!). A guy tells me I can sell it in Delhi. It could make a small mountain of rupees.

The next day, I told a French friend about it. We decided to go together. Anyway, Manali's climate was too cold and humid at the moment.

We pass through Kullu again and exchange a few words with the baba of the small temple, using gestures and the little Hindi we know. He speaks more to me and makes me understand that he would be happy if I came to his temple, in the travelers' section, and that I welcome Westerners passing through. I am touched, as I was in Banares with the fire baba. I tell him I will come back.

The journey to Delhi is going very well. We cross Punjab, India's breadbasket. It is as green as Rajasthan is yellow.

One evening, we arrive in a small town. We look for a place to sleep, we find a park that looks very welcoming. We sit there and before sleeping we make ourselves a chillum. Opposite us, there are two guys watching us. We invite them to smoke. They approach and puff on the chillum. And then, one of them decides to touch my feet, as a sign of respect. Ouch, I'm really bothered. Not because he bows down, that had already happened to me during my walks around Manali and elsewhere, but because he stays for a long time touching my feet. I tell him half in English, half in Hindi to get up, that he doesn't have to bow down like that,

7 years on the road

but nothing doing, he doesn't move. And it goes on! I can see that he's fed up. He's on his knees and starting to suffer, finally, he lies flat on his stomach while continuing to touch my feet. I try to tell him to stop - nicely anyway, but nothing works. After a very long time, I'm fed up and I'm about to lift him up by force by the shoulder, but I've barely touched him, when he stands up, relieved. So, there you go, I've just discovered that all it takes is touching his shoulder to put an end to this prostration.

We're on a truck that picked us up. It goes to Delhi, but not New Delhi. And there, the misery hits us. Thousands of people live on the sidewalk. Without mats, without anything. What strikes me most are the widows with their children. They only own a few pots and pans and sleep around them. I'd been told that, but I didn't believe it.

The truck stops for a bite to eat, I suppose. It's on a small street where lots of men dressed in white are chatting among themselves. We stay on the truck.

They're all armed with clubs, like pickaxe handles. They're strikers. They're coming back from a demonstration. They laugh, gently mocking us, and start hitting the truck with clubs, saying "hippies[1]." It makes them laugh. And then little by little, the blows become more and more frequent, and some of them try to hit us. A big, laughing cop, his rifle slung over his shoulder, doesn't move. That's when I start to get worried. My friend does too. But luckily, a good guy, clearly respected by the protesters, intervenes, and the others stop. Phew! We didn't come far. Non-violent people can get seriously off the rails when they're in a group.

Luckily, the driver returns and we head back to New Delhi. It's not late. We rush to get my ticket refunded. It's open. I go there, my friend is waiting outside. But then, disappointment, too late, the ticket is expired by a week or two.

Too bad. The near-renouncer that I am is punished. You renounce or you don't renounce, you have to choose. When I go out, I find my friend in great shape and smiling, sitting on the ground in front of his open lota. I tell him that for me, it's ruined. And he shows me a handful of rupees. Twenty-dollar bills. For us, it's a small fortune. He explains to me that while I was at the agency, he had his lota in

---

[1] I'm still in jeans.

7 years on the road

front of him, open just in case, and that an American emptied his pockets of all his Indian money. He couldn't stand India anymore and was heading back to the West.

Without question, we rush to the lassis vendors and gorge ourselves on barfis, mango lassis, sugarcane juice... We buy all the gluttony that tempts us and that we haven't eaten since our arrival in India. We make the small street vendors happy, whether they're on the streets or not.

And then we'll throw it all up in the first discreet corner. Pathetic!

We split up, my friend is heading towards Varanasi and I'm heading back towards Manali. I'm going to cross Punjab quietly and discover the Sikhs. It's not really my route, but I want to wander around. It's truly a fertile area. A prosperous state. It feels like the countryside in Western Europe. It's nice to see. Plus, the locals are very welcoming. The first night, I sleep in a Sikh temple at the invitation of the faithful. There's only one rule: no tobacco or anything related to the idea of smoking. They show me an outdoor spot on the temple wall between two stones. It bothers me a little, but I leave my Charas and my tobacco. They've noticed my excitement and reassure me. No one will touch it.

Indeed, it's still there the next morning. Thanks guys!

The second day I arrive in a small town. Right away, a guy in his twenties invites me into his home. This is quite rare in India. But I understand. He's a Christian. We don't discuss religion much. A little, though. He feels a little lonely, drowned in turbans and long or coiled beards held in place by a net attached to his ears.

The next day, for my departure, he gave me an animal skin that I took for a polar bear skin until a few years ago, now I have a doubt[1], but I don't see what else it could be. The skin was small but very hairy, very thick. I thank him warmly. I am proud of it, I imagine myself as Shiva on his tiger skin, according to the images on the calendars distributed by Indian traders.

---

[1] It was too small.

7 years on the road

I still have a hell of a way to go. By chance, if it exists, I meet a very bearded American. We chat a little about what he's doing in the USA. He owns a small shop in California, and he's earned enough money to pay for his trip in comfortable conditions. The shop runs without him thanks to a temporary manager, and every month, he earns enough to continue traveling. He's just hired a taxi to go to Simla. He offers me to come with him, which I accept with great pleasure. We agree on an arrangement: in Simla, he pays for a hotel room for me, food too, of course, and the next day, we each go our separate ways. That suits me just fine.

Simla is Switzerland. High mountains and fir trees everywhere. I have a great night's sleep and am one of the first people in the village to wake up. During the night, dozens of large, aggressive monkeys, apparently baboons, have taken over the town. Frankly, I don't feel reassured at all, but gradually Simla awakens. The monkeys eventually give way to the humans.

I thank my American. And I set off for Kullu and Manali. The weather has improved, but it rains often. Perhaps it's the monsoon. But I take shelter because I don't want to damage my polar bear skin—if that's what it is.

Since leaving Delhi, I have given up trousers and sweaters, and have resumed my longi and the piece of cotton I wear on my shoulders.

I return to Kullu and happily meet my favorite baba. He renews his offer to welcome visiting Westerners in the designated part of the temple. I tell him I'll come soon. Then I continue on to Manali. Why? It's silly. Perhaps it's because I want to talk, to communicate more easily.

7 years on the road

I stay in Manali for a while, I don't remember how long. It's cold and damp, we eat what we can. It rains all the time. I meet up with the Niçois gang, the junkies who were rampant in Morocco. I stay for a week or two, wondering what I'm doing there. I meet a junkie friend who has rented a house. I move in with him for about a week, during which the rain doesn't stop. We shoot up opium. When the rain stops, I'm very vaguely addicted, for half an hour, but I don't really feel any withdrawal.

And then I'm fed up with all these Westerners. I'm no better than them. Occasionally, I take a few walks around the area. I even go as far as Dharamsala. It's a quiet city, I go to a square supposedly where the Buddha remained for twenty years meditating under a tree. But I'm probably wrong, because there's nothing to indicate it. No Buddhists, no temple, nothing at all. And maybe I'm not in Dharamsala.

One day, I found myself in the mountains with a French colleague and a sâdhu. We arrived at the home of a very poor peasant. He invited us to eat, and beforehand, after rinsing our hands, he washed our feet. Although I told him it was fine, he insisted and did it well. And he was very happy. For him, it was good for his next reincarnation.

Around Manali, along the roadsides, there are many Tibetan refugees. Some run restaurants. Their only dish is thick boiled and fried spaghetti, served with cabbage leaves cooked the same way. Nothing else. No sauce, no lassi. Nothing. They are very poor.

A little further on, there are some people selling Chang—rice beer, to be drunk directly from a kettle, through the spout. It's not bad, and it's a bit intoxicating. But, well, I'm wasting my time here.

I feel like leaving. So I'm leaving. Heading to Kullu, where I intend to spend some time.

7 years on the road

7 years on the road

The Kullu small temple

The baba greets me silently. He has people in his courtyard and wants to stay in character. He makes it clear that I'm the boss in the visitor reception area. I settle down on my bearskin. I remain calm and relaxed, sitting cross-legged. I appreciate this calm and silence. The river flows about thirty meters in front of me. We can clearly see the mark of the last cremation.

Since then, a more complete temple has been built over the old one

The place is superb. The baba comes to see me, his guests have left, it's getting dark. He brings some rudimentary dishes and wood. I make a fire. He goes back to get a chillum. We each smoke it in turn. Not bad at all. He tries to make me understand that his Charas comes from Nepal. I make him taste my Manali, the one I made myself. When night falls, he leaves.

7 years on the road

There are people passing through this temple. Practically every day. A few Westerners on their way to Manali and quite a few sadhus in transit. I keep the fire lit. I'm proud, even if it's not my usual temperament. I manage, with varying degrees of success, to ensure that everyone has something to eat and smoke. As for smoking, it's fine, but as for eating, that's more complicated, since I don't have a penny. We manage as best we can, with the people passing through.

I noticed, quite quickly, that the temple baba goes out at night and comes back completely drunk. He swears like a carter as he falls out of bed. I don't know where he goes to drink, but it must be discreet. On the other hand, his return is not at all. But, every morning, he is as fresh as a daisy and puffs on his chillum quietly, facing the river. When he is available, he comes to see me and the passengers and we smoke very good Charas.

Today, a cremation is taking place. It's a far cry from the Mediterranean tears and hysteria. The family members are keeping a little to themselves. The pile of wood is very high and located on the riverbank. The temple baba sits on his heels, tugging at his chillum, as a spectator. I'm watching the ceremony. The family is rather calm except for one of the sons, dressed in Western clothes, who feels compelled to cry loudly. The fire is crackling. I lose interest for some reason. When I return, people are no longer there, and the temple baba collects the unburned wood. It has become sacred wood and will join the sacred fire.

One morning, the baba comes to see me with enormous tailor's shears and a tiny piece of what looks like photographic film. There is a Westerner with me. The baba manages to cut the piece of film into three, which appears to be an Acid called "window open"—I'm not at all sure of the name, let alone its spelling. It's the Westerner who explains this to me.

Wrong move, one piece falls into the sacred fire. The baba makes a gesture to the Westerner who is still sitting next to the fire. He basically says, "Sorry, but it's your part that fell." And we take the two remaining pieces.
And there, I find what I felt in Morocco and Tunisia, at night under the stars. There, it's day. No anxiety. I am completely in communion with the world, while still having the other me who appreciates what the first me does or does not do. It may be difficult to understand, but that's it. The intensity is such that everything

7 years on the road

is explained, everything is understood, and it's absolutely impossible to say or describe. I walk around the temple and its surroundings, a big smile on my lips.

The woodpile was at least 3 times higher than this one

Suddenly, I hear something like a gunshot. It doesn't bother me at all, but I go to look at the river anyway. There's a cop accompanying a prisoner wearing handcuffs. And, boom, another gunshot. In fact, it's the baba, laughing, throwing fire crackers at them, like Western kids. He's crying with laughter. The cop doesn't appreciate it too much, but the baba is sacred. So, he decides to move faster. And then, it must be said that the river is sacred, more than the others, since it is mentioned in the Rig Veda[1]. The temple is also sacred. So, the space between the two is also sacred. So the cop who was dragging his prisoner wasn't respecting the place.

A little later, I see a sâdhu arrive, quite old, with a disciple. Babas don't usually have disciples. However, I'm intrigued because the sâdhu, who looks more like a swami dressed all in orange, seems blond to me. Time stands still, and I tell myself that this swami is a Westerner. He must have been in India for a long time. I look at him intensely. He does the same. And then he says to me: "From witch country do you belong?" And I burst out laughing. What's more, he said it with

---

[1]Since then it has changed its name and is called Beas.

the accent of those from Bombay. Seen up close, he has white hair and looks like a professional guru. He's probably not a crook. But he doesn't mind my reaction and sits down facing the river and the mountain. He meditates.

I continue to have experiences in this temple. I get along well with the baba. And time has stopped. This leads me to ask myself questions, including this one: Does time really pass? Does it really exist?

How long did I stay in that temple? At least two months, I think. Two months of peace and happiness.

One day, while I was making a chillum, on my little white bear, or supposedly one, I looked up and, great surprise, my latest girlfriend who came straight from Brittany was standing in front of me. Super sexy in her tight jeans and her t-shirt sticking to her enormous free chest, which must have driven the Indians crazy, she was standing right in front of me.

Actually, it was planned. I was even the one who asked her to join me in India be fore leaving. But I didn't really believe it or care. And now, frankly, it bothers me a little, even a lot. I had completely forgotten about her. I'm light years away from wanting to experience a romance.

But, well, I'm leaving the temple for a few days. We go to the hotel where nothing happens, even though I was rather inclined to do so when I first met her, and we part quickly. She goes to Delhi and continues her stay in India on her own, with an American she met in Mumbai, and I return to the small temple. I still feel a certain embarrassment and my conscience is not entirely clear, but I am very happy to be back at the temple.

One thing intrigues me, though: how did she find me? She'll never tell me, even when I find her again upon my return. A little anecdote to note: one evening in a dive, an Indian offered to buy or rent her.

At the temple, life returns to normal. But I'm starting to get some diarrhea. Noth ing serious at first, but it's strange that it's happening to me now. I'm finding it harder and harder to keep down what I eat. The "turista" strikes at the beginning of a change of scenery, not several months later. I ask myself the question: Why here? Why now?

It's getting more and more annoying. While wandering around Kullu, I discover an open-air restaurant serving cooked liver. It reminds me of my childhood and the calf's liver my mother used to make. This one must not be veal. I try it and find it delicious. No more vegetarianism! I'm too sick for that.

I discover a truck that's distributing free cartons of milk. The guy throws them into the crowd, who try to catch them. I do the same and enjoy myself. Well, it doesn't change anything for the diarrhea, quite the opposite, but it's good, and that's already good.

7 years on the road

7 years on the road

A little blonde, a kitten and...

One morning, I wake up and see several people sleeping. They are Westerners who arrived during the night. I see this in the sleeping bags. Little by little, they open and heads appear. And then, I have a shock: Michel shows his nose. Yes, it is indeed the Michel who was with me in Africa. I am happy to see him again. He doesn't seem surprised. He must have recognized me when I was sleeping. He is not alone in his sleeping bag. A small, clean-cut blonde girl, with makeup on her eyes, a small black cat in her hand, appears in the sleeping bag.

Lots of things happen in life! While the water heats, I prepare the first chillum of the day. Michel is going to Manali. He wants to buy a kilo of hashish to sell in Delhi. I think it's an excellent idea and naturally, I go with him, I even suggest that he go and sell it in Banares. But, the little blonde doesn't like that. I suppose she's the one who holds the purse strings, if not the purse itself.

I greet the baba one last time and leave this small temple with a strange feeling, almost of guilt.

Arriving in Manali, we split up. The blonde and her cat went to a hotel, while Michel and I set off on a hunt in the mountains. We finally arrived at a house, a sort of chalet, where several Indians were staying. One of them set off to collect the best of the best: rolls of fresh charas, hand-rolled by the local farmers.

And then we wait quietly. Michel negotiated the price. I'm not interested. And then, in this "chalet" lost in the mountains, a group of French people arrive, including one I knew well in Morocco. They're junkies. They offer us a morphine fix. We're not too keen, they insist, so okay for a small one, not too strong, so as not to offend them.

7 years on the road

Oh! Luckily the high isn't too strong; I vomit everything I've eaten. Michel too. But once we get past this, a great sense of well-being reigns within us. My intestinal problems disappear. We remain facing the valley, sitting cross-legged without speaking. We no longer feel concerned by anything. Shortly after, the guy who had gone to get the rolls of resin returns.

Hand-rolled Charas balls and rolls

It takes a second look for us to realize he's back with a kilo of charas. We don't check. Michel pays him, we thank him, and we leave. Luckily, he had haggled over the price before taking the morphine shot.

Back to Manali. Once the morphine wears off, my guts wake up. Now I know how to stop the tourista, but I know the ravages of morphine and I don't want to fall for it. I talk about it with the friend who fixed my passport. He tells me the only way not to die right away is to swallow a small ball of opium. It blocks the intestines for about ten hours. Small doses like that don't make you addicted right away. He gives me a good piece and breaks off a fragment that he rolls into a ball. It must be about three or four millimeters in diameter. Sure enough, I vomit first, and the little that has been digested blocks my intestines.

7 years on the road

I'm back with Michel, his little girlfriend, and his black cat. Our first step is to find the best part of the kilo and keep it for ourselves. I find about fifty grams, which I put aside in a small cloth bag tied with a small cotton cord. I keep this tiny bag with me. Michel puts the rest of the kilo in his travel bag, the same one he had in Africa.

We decide on a plan. We take the train to Delhi. There, I turn off for Banares, where they're supposed to meet me, and I wait for them to finish their work.

We're approaching Delhi by train; it's the first time I've paid, or more precisely, someone has paid for me. At a stop in a small station, three uniformed cops quickly get on. They rush toward me, tell me to raise my hands. One of them searches me. He finds the small bag. He turns to his colleagues and says, "Ah, hippies!" All three of them get back off, and the train leaves immediately. The driver must be in on the scam. The hold-up only lasted thirty seconds. Michel is still sitting on his bag with his kilo inside. The worst is avoided, but the Indian cops are still full of nerve. In all my travels, this is the first time I've actually been robbed. In India, by cops! It gives you an idea of the corruption that reigns in the world's largest democracy.

I get off at Hardwar, which is to the east. I find the cops a bit too dangerous to continue by train; I still have a good piece of Nepalese that I had in a small metal box in my cotton bag. I walk a short distance, which is still killing me. I'm out of opium and I don't want to smoke Charas. Michel will be here for a while, according to what he told me, so I'm going to see my sâdhu friends in the big park.

There are even more than last time. I don't see any familiar faces apart from the one staring at the sun. However, a small group gives me the sign of the mixture of tobacco and Charas. I nod and join them and take out my Nepalese. The "Bom Shankar[1]!" resound and the chillums spin. But, I'm not as enthusiastic as before. And yet, I like my babas. It's mutual: apart from the hashish I bring them: I have the right reflexes to be around them, I don't ask questions, I consider them at their true worth, I live barefoot and completely deprived of everything. I will never be one of them, because I am a Westerner, and that is impossible to change. But they like me. It's mutual and I realize that I like that they like me.

---

[1] This cry is the most famous of the cries that sadhus utter before smoking, addressing it to the god Shiva. (Shankara = who makes happiness)

7 years on the road

I walk along the river, where everyone goes to defecate. A liter of black water falls between my feet. It stinks! I have to find a solution, otherwise I feel like I won't live long. I mention it, with gestures and a few words of Hindi, to the baba who is cooking the rice. He signals to me that the cooking water is what's needed. He also shows me a small box, like a big matchbox, filled with rice bran. I still have my doubts. If it's normal diarrhea, it might be enough to block it, but if it's amoebas, I'm done for. Considering what I've just expelled, I'd still prefer an opium pellet.

Of course, the idea of returning to Brittany comes to me. But I don't want to leave India. And Michel is due to join me in a few weeks in Banares.

I have no opium, and my diarrhea is getting worse and worse. I empty myself completely. So I leave the babas a good piece of Nepalese and head for Agra, where I know I can find opium without having to look for.

I arrive in Agra. The journey has been very difficult. I'm completely out of opium, and diarrhea strikes me at any time. When it comes, I clench my buttocks and wait to find a corner. Soon, I won't be able to hold it in any longer.

Stock up on opium. It's not free, but it's really cheap, enough for the few rupees Michel gave me. The individual ball costs 10 paesas[1]. I put a good piece in my iron box, like a shoe polish box that already contains my Nepalese. And I wrap the rest in paper covered with cotton cloth.

Behind the Taj Mahal, the small temple is still there, and there are a bunch of Westerners chatting with Sri Kahn Baba. Oddly enough, he's fascinated by what a beautiful woman sitting next to him is saying. He manages to look away from his slightly open Indian shirt, smile at me, and tell me to sit down. I take out a piece of Nepalese and "Bom Shankar!" Here we go again. The little ball of opium I swallowed at the shop is having its effect. My guts are quieting down, and I feel much better. It's probably the effect of the opium. The ball wasn't big, but fresher than anything I'd tasted before. I feel good, in my head and in my body. But, I risk becoming an addict, and I don't want that. I've seen enough junkies...

---

[1] Ten cents of rupees.

7 years on the road

I had a wonderful night, but the urge to defecate returned, and I walked away from the temple along the Yamuna. I was astounded by the amount of black water I was ejecting. And yet, I had barely eaten anything.

The next day, I go to the other side of the Taj Mahal, still along the river, to the mini-village a few hundred meters away. There are dogs everywhere. They're fat and all have alopecia. Monsters.

Back at the temple, I see a girl shouting in English. She points to the Yamuna. A body floating in the water. Fully clothed. A poor man. A snack for stray dogs. It's strange, but it's the custom. The Yamuna is sacred. So it's good for the poor man's karma; he'll be less so in his next reincarnation. The baba confirms this to us. The corpse remains for several days in front of the temple because there are no currents there.

For my part, I try to find a formula so that the food I eat nourishes me, and is not rejected. Chai[1] is fine. Bananas too, but that's it.

I get into the habit of going to the mini-village to drink my tea and eat a banana after the evening emptying, while the opium pellet takes effect. I also meet a few Westerners from whom I ask for a little money. It works quite well. they must have pity on me.

That evening, it was already dark, I stayed to chat at the chai shop, a little with some Indians over a chai — tea — and then we split up and I returned to the temple by the usual route, that is to say behind the Taj Mahal, along the Yamuna. Since Hardwar I've been moving with a stick to help me walk. Luckily I have it. But it's not enough.

Three or four dogs start circling me. I feel like trouble is coming. And they attack. They try to jump on me. I hit as hard as I can, but I feel like I won't get the upper hand. The club doesn't scare them. They take it on as part of me and try to bite it. I have to change tactics, or they'll eat me. I quickly pick up a few stones and throw them at them. Good idea, they don't understand what's happening to them. They keep their distance. But I shoot pretty well and arrive at the temple in one piece.

---

[1] Indian tea, boiled and served in milk.

7 years on the road

Friendly stray dog.

The next day, I'm in awful shape. In the evening, a group of Westerners arrives, completely panicked. They tell us the cops are coming and that they want to hide five kilos of Charas. The baba refuses and points them to the river. It's pitch black. But they go. Four or five plainclothes cops burst into the temple. One asks for my passport. I show it to him. He notices that the second stamp[1] isn't up to date. The other one, the one my friend reviewed and corrected in Manali, is fine. I don't worry; the opium takes over. So I'm very calm and very relaxed. The cop tells me he'll update it and leaves with two of his colleagues, the others rush into the night, along the Yamuna. The baba hasn't said anything. This temple isn't a train station concourse. If the temple had been guarded by the main baba of Varanasi, or even any real baba, the cops wouldn't have dared. But we're dealing with a fake baba, a son of a good family with long hair who only thinks about screwing American women who come to spend some time in the shadow of the Taj Mahal.

---

[1] This is a stamp that specifies that the passport holder must report to a police station on the date indicated, which corresponds to that of the other stamp.

7 years on the road

The cops come back, I'm still not worried. Mine gives me back my passport. I check. Indeed, he has corrected the problem. I pick up the passport and thank him. And then, he panics and demands that I pay the taxes. Oh, I should have thought of that! I ask him how much. He tells me twenty rupees. Exactly what I have, not a paesa more. I give him my ticket, he thanks me, and leaves. The largest democracy in the world has a very greedy police force.

I'm still in Agra. My condition is stable. That is to say, in the morning, I go to empty myself along the river, where everyone else does, to the great delight of the stray dogs. I swallow my opium pellet. And off I go for the day feeling pretty good. I'll drink a lassi when I can. I don't throw it up. That's something. I'll have to go to Banares because Michel and his little girlfriend are going to show up one of these days. And I'd really like to see the babas again. But I doubt they'll still be there.

Well! One morning, I decide to leave. This time, I find the road long and arduous. Hitchhiking doesn't work very well. On the other hand, the hippies and tourists I ask for a little money are scared to see me, and so they're quite generous.
Finally, I arrive in Varanasi. The problem is, I don't feel strong enough to cross the city. Too bad, I have to go. I wait until evening anyway, until the streets calm down, relatively speaking. I take several breaks. Finally, I arrive at the ghat. The temple nearby is still ringing its cymbals and bells. There are several babas in circles, some alone, others meditating, or resting, peacefully. I go to wash my feet in the Ganges. It's brown, I see a turd passing a meter from me. There are lots of Hindus washing and performing ablutions. I don't know where I'm going to sleep. On the ghat? Luckily, I still have my bearskin. It cushions the contact between my bones and the cement.

The night is hard. There are a lot of people passing by, and I'm worried about a possible raid by the police. Because my visa, even if it's faked, is no longer valid at all. I've heard about renting a houseboat. There are several moored at the bottom of the ghat. The price is ridiculous, so I rent one for a week.

I only last two days. I can feel the dampness seeping through the wood. I'm reaching the following extremely painful situation: I can neither lie down, nor sit, nor stand. The opium helps me, but I mustn't become addicted. And for that, there's only one solution: take only small pellets. Especially not inject it or smoke it.

I search for a solution while walking in the streets near the ghat. The smells, which I used to like so much, now disgust me. At the turn of a street, I run into a Frenchman who sees my state and invites me into the house he's renting with three or four other guys. Finally, a bed. It's far from ideal, but it's a quiet house, and it does me a world of good. But I still have trouble sleeping. One of them finds a solution: a Mandrax[1] in the evening. I saw this in Goa, when a guy who was having a bad trip was evacuated. It's the only way to stop someone who's freaking out in the middle of a trip. It should put me to sleep. And indeed, it works.

In the evening when I decide to sleep, I swallow my Mandrax, go take a shower on the other side of the yard, go back to my bed, and fall asleep immediately.

It's amazing how good it makes me feel. I'm still in a terrible state, but I have a bed, a shower, and I sleep.

I realize I'm at the end of my rope. I can't live here for one good reason: I'm not Indian. I don't belong here. I'm a Westerner. I'm not rejecting anything about Indian spirituality; I simply realize that I don't belong. I have to go home. I'm Breton, so I must be in Brittany. Logical.

I start thinking about the embankments, the fields of my native Brittany. I think about the sea, the rain, the wind, the heather flowers, the green meadows and the apple trees in bloom. Good God, what am I doing here eating bananas, dragging my carcass around. I'm dying to eat buckwheat pancakes with buttermilk, fried potatoes, meadows... I miss my country so much that all I can think about is it. Goodbye babas, goodbye Shiva! After 10 months in India, it's time to send out an SOS. I write to my parents that I'm going home. I plan to go via Iran where Westerners like me can work on a construction site. They tell me they're sending me a plane ticket and that I'll find it in Delhi, at the French consulate. Honestly, that suits me.

---

[1] Ultra powerful sleeping pill.

7 years on the road

My parents sent me a 100-franc note on a folded sheet of carbon paper, mailed inside the letter. So I took the train to Delhi, in third class, of course.

The train is jammed. Worse than anything I've ever seen of its kind. I manage to climb onto a wooden luggage rack above the passengers. Completely pleased with myself, I don't move. But after a while, I need to pee, and there's no way I'm going to the bathroom: the corridor is full of passengers, the toilets too, and in any case, inaccessible. And at that moment, the train stops in the middle of the night in the open countryside. So I decide to climb out the window. Outside, it's pitch black. It's deserted. Not a house, no one. Just as I've finished peeing, the train starts up again. I rush to the window and try to climb back up using my arms, but I'm far too weak, and there I am, alone, in my longi, in the middle of the desert... But luckily, a passenger grabs me by the arms and pulls me up as if I weighed nothing. Phew!!!!!!

Indian Train 1947. Not much had changed.

At the consulate, they find me some old clothes and put me in the waiting room, which everyone carefully avoids. I stay for a few days while my plane ticket arrives. There, I meet a Breton woman from Central Brittany who has come to de-

7 years on the road

clare the death of her 5-year-old son, Mathias. I had met them in Goa and Manali. A nice little boy. It's a shock.

On the plane, when the flight attendant asks me what I want to eat and if I want to drink something, I order a Ricard, red wine, and all the food from all the stops, and of course I throw up everything.
It's snowing when I arrive at Orly[1].

---

[1] Paris airport.

7 years on the road

Degemer mat e Breizh[1].

When I arrived in Brittany, I weighed only 50 kg for 1.83 meters tall. But, in fact, it was more fear than harm. It was Endonymax Nana, or more simply amoebas, that almost killed me. The family doctor who treated me was deported during the war. He saw the concentration camp survivors drop like flies when the liberators arrived and rushed to get food. He only prescribed me baby food, and I slowly re covered under the attentive care of my mother, happy to see me come back alive. Let's not forget that I had gone to India to end my days there (at 25!). As for drugs, I'm not addicted to anything. Everything's fine on that front.

Brittany is in turmoil. It's the end of 1973, and Breton national sentiment has been reawakening for several years. This is fortunate, because I've returned from Banares more Breton than ever. I'm in awe of my country. I find it magnificent. When my health recovers fairly quickly, I ate, during a family visit near Paimpol, a meal of scallops in cream sauce that impresses everyone.

In fact, I felt Breton, not French, from my youth. I discovered, while reading The White Wolf by Paul Féval, that Brittany had been independent and had fought to remain so. For me, it was a surprise, because it was a taboo subject at the time. I was completely shocked.

I had been closely following the Le Goarnig family's troubles with the French government, which refused to recognize the first names of their fourteen children —Breton names, of course. I would have the opportunity to meet them later.

And then one day, my father announced that he had found me a job. Selling life insurance door-to-door in Saint-Malo. Quite unconsciously, I accepted, and I found myself in a suit and moped, crisscrossing the council estates, trying to sell these products, which were almost a scam.

---
[1]Welcome to Brittany.

7 years on the road

Obviously, it was a rotten job, where employees, on a six-month trial period, insured their entire family and friends. After six months, they weren't making their money and left on their own. Luckily for me, I didn't play that game and I managed to sell enough insurance to live as best I could.

I have no business sense, but I do have sympathy, which means I almost become friends with the people I approach.

But I don't like it. I still have the distinct impression that I'm ripping them off. I have no friends, no girlfriend, no TV, no car (or license), in short, I'm bored. And then one day, still canvassing, I come across people very close to me. I could have found them in India or Morocco. We become friends. They have hash from time to time, we smoke together and very quickly, the need to leave becomes clear.

We were in the midst of the spectacular attacks by the Brittany Liberation Front. A large part of the Breton population was in favor of it, even after the destruction of the Roch Trédudon pylon in February 1974, which deprived Lower Brittany of television. It seems unthinkable now, but at the time, many people applauded. Especially young people who were "against television."

But, well, I'm content to provide moral support. One day, I discover Gilles Servat's "White Ermine" on the jukebox of the café where I meet my employers. It's a real shock.

My darling says it's crazy
to go to war with the Franks
But I say it's madness
to be chained longer
Here she is, the White Hermine.... etc.

But, I have a burning desire to get back on the road. One of my friends has a plan to go to the French Riviera to sell ice cream on the beaches. It doesn't pay well, but I'm interested. I'm fed up with this job with its dubious morality, and I decide to go with him. He has a car, so I don't have to hitchhike, which is a big change.

7 years on the road

It's worth noting, however, that my employers don't want to let me go, and even bring down a specialist in difficult cases from Rennes. It's a waste of time; I'm leaving with the satisfaction of having stood up to a tough guy.

There are about a dozen of us young people working for the same company in Le Lavandou. The boss allocates the beaches based on our means of transport. I'm the only pedestrian, and he assigns me the town's municipal beach. The others share the small, discreet beaches in the surrounding area. On mine, I have twelve competitors selling ice cream, of course, but also doughnuts and other things I can't remember.

I do my job conscientiously, but the takings aren't great. Our group has a natural leader. A big, burly, hairy, bearded guy who comes every year. He's a Maoist and has a vision of things that I like: It's not normal that those who have a car earn significantly more than those who don't. So, the leader suggests that all the takings be added up and then divided equally. That suits me, because I'm far from being favored with this frenzied competition.

Summer is coming to an end, and I decide to go to work in Switzerland. They're looking for apricot and other produce pickers. That suits me.

So I'm back on the road, as I loved to do so much: alone. I'm taking my time, I've got the last paycheck for ice cream, it's a bit of a change, and it's no worse than being broke, because in terms of hospitality, France is far from being worth the same as poor countries.

These are great moments, for me at least, these walks through the Alps of Haute-Provence. Hitchhiking doesn't work much, but I'm in no hurry, and the weather is nice. I even stop at a hotel and go to the movies. Luxury, what else!

I was advised to go to Saxon, between Lausanne and Sion, so I went there. No problem finding work. Off the books, of course. There were about thirty of us, in cluding quite a few Bretons, but also Quebecers, Americans in minibuses, and English. The atmosphere was nice. We smoked a little from time to time. We also drank occasionally in the evening. I did a whole bunch of odd jobs. I picked apri cots, cauliflowers, tomatoes, grapes. I became a roofer's assistant for half a day, and then a baker's assistant. I worked for a month in the main bakery in Saxon,

7 years on the road

and I decided to return to Brittany. The pay wasn't great, but when it came time to exchange money, it was multiplied by 3.5. Opulence! So I decided to return by train, first class!
But this time, I'm not leaving. I'm staying in Brittany.

50 years later

Almost to the day, I finished translating the Rig Veda. I live in the heart of central Brittany. I have a small house with a garden in a small village, far from everything. I receive the minimum old-age pension, and that suits me very well.

It took me six years to translate the Rig Veda, which is, for me, an achievement. With my professional aptitude certificate, I was far from the classical Sanskritists and, fortunately for me, I didn't have the certainties they obtained from the begin ning of their studies: the Rig Veda was brought to Indians by Westerners 3,500 years ago.

While translating, I also discovered that the Rig Veda was THE book – oral, of course – of the 7 Rivers civilization, which we know better as the Indus civilization.

This civilization was the opposite of ours, the one that reigns over the entire planet, with local variations, of course. Ours is pyramidal. Vertical, as they say now. At the very top, regardless of the country, the regime, the mode of operation, a tiny minority reigns, deciding everything, enriching itself as much as pos sible, and at the bottom, the people try to survive.

Our globalized civilization will do as all those that preceded it: it will end.

In seven years, I discovered peoples and cultures completely different from the one I had been raised in. I was angry with the Western world and with the destiny reserved for me. I wanted to see peoples, individuals, who did not think like Europeans.

Everywhere, whether in India, North Africa or sub-Saharan Africa, I met simple, open, hospitable and above all very friendly people, with a few rare and inevitable exceptions.

7 years on the road

It was the opposite of Europe, where you also find people of the same type, but much more rarely. Westerners are ethnocentric, that is, they believe that their way of life, their morals, their values, their beliefs are the only good ones and that the rest of the world should think like them. They consider themselves superior and have ravaged the planet, destroyed cultures, and committed the worst atrocities in the name of civilization, the love of God, and even in the name of human rights.

It is ideology that destroys the natural, fraternal feeling of humanity toward its fellow human beings. The life I have led during these seven years has introduced me to people of all colors, cultures, and religions, and, except for a few cases, I have only met kind, helpful, generous, and supportive people.
Unfortunately, the few exceptions I mentioned above take advantage of the natural goodness of these peoples to steal from them, exploit them and set them against each other, in the name of ideologies, each more questionable than the last.

Man is naturally good, as Rousseau said, with exceptions, of course. The more wealth he accumulates, the less good he is. The most striking example is the ordinary Westerner who believes himself superior to the rest of humanity because he has developed technical mastery and accumulated wealth.

But, nowadays, we see that this era is over. The white man no longer rules the world. The expulsion of France from its former African colonies is a perfect example. The election of Donald Trump is another. The rallying of multi-billionaires to his brutal and openly fascist policies is a surge of those who sense the end of their world domination. Greed and selfishness reign over the most powerful country in the world. A war will soon break out between the countries of Western Europe and Russia over more than dubious border issues. Some politicians think this is the best way to enter history. Nothing like a good old war to leave your name for future generations? Of course, the leaders won't be on the front lines, but the 19-year-colds, yes...

But nature intervenes. It takes revenge for what man has done to it. Global warming is causing natural disaster after natural disaster. Floods, megafires, melting glaciers, and therefore rising sea levels, hurricanes, are occurring at an ever-increasing pace.

7 years on the road

Our materialistic, greedy, globalized civilization will have to stop whether we like it or not. It will have to change profoundly, because in less than two centuries, we have exhausted the natural resources that allow us to live as we do now. We have destroyed our soils to produce ever more, polluted our waterways, exhausted our mines and all non-renewable energy sources. Whether we like it or not, we will no longer be able to live as before.

As temperatures rise, viruses follow the heat, and soon the Ebola virus[1], which has wreaked so much havoc in Africa, will come to us. In 2020, we experienced the Covid-19 pandemic, a small virus that killed few people and paralyzed the planet. With Ebola, it will be a different story.

Everything we do is accelerating global warming, and therefore the disasters it causes. Today, as I write these lines, almost half of Brittany is flooded. And the peak has not yet been reached.

But that's nothing compared to melting glaciers. They raise sea levels. Those in Greenland and Antarctica are particularly threatening. The one in West Antarctica, which is melting from below, if it fractures and falls into the sea, would suddenly raise sea levels by 3 to 6 meters, depending on the studies and the type of fracturing. This means that all the planet's ports would be underwater. All maritime traffic would be forced to stop.
If these glaciers don't fall into the water, they will continue to melt. The level will continue to rise, more slowly but just as surely, causing entire countries to disappear.

A massive fire nearly destroyed Los Angeles a week or two ago. It was widely covered on television because of the stars who lived there. But it was nothing compared to the megafires destroying the rest of California, the Amazon, and other forests (Greece, Congo, Australia, Canada, etc.).
This global warming will lead to massive migrations of people living near the equator to cooler areas. Racists and xenophobes, who are multiplying at the head of Western states and among the population, can build all the walls they want, but they won't be able to stop anything.

---

[1] And many more.

7 years on the road

Intensive agriculture has killed biodiversity. Our soils are almost dead, and with out massive fertilizer inputs, harvests would be ridiculous. People will kill for food.

The water tables are emptying. Even in flooded Brittany, the aquifers are not full. In Punjab, India, poverty has replaced opulence. This region, once so green, no longer has water in its aquifers. This is leading the governments of India, China, and Pakistan to develop dam projects in the Himalayas, which are regularly shaken by earthquakes, risking causing gigantic humanitarian disasters.

If we add to this soil erosion, as in the American Midwest, famines will develop, resulting in, among other things, mass migrations.

Can we prevent it?

All these catastrophes will go hand in hand with a collapse of the globalized financial system. Money will be worthless. The global debt is $100 trillion. Every thing could collapse overnight. Crises and revolts will multiply. The repression of regimes, all increasingly authoritarian, will claim mountains of victims.

We're all dependent on electricity. All it would take is a solar storm, like the one in 1859, for everything to stop working. We wouldn't even be able to start our cars.

Everything is computerized and dematerialized. A massive internet outage would cause a global, economic, and social disaster.

Wars between major powers have already begun all over the planet, for now, through small proxy countries like Ukraine. But never since the dawn of human ity have weapons been so sophisticated. Nuclear bombs can no longer be tested in real-life situations. Those at Hiroshima and Nagasaki are largely outdated. Ex perts are unaware of the power of the new bombs.

Inequality has never been so pronounced. Millions of people are dying of hunger or cold, while the super-rich don't know what to do with their money.
Solidarity and mutual aid are becoming outdated values. They have been replaced by exacerbated individualism, unbridled consumption, and the loss of tra

7 years on the road

ditional social ties. The consequences are an increase in depression, suicide among young people in the wealthiest countries, and a rise in mental illnesses such as narcissistic perversion.

The list is unfortunately not complete. Our future is rather bleak, but there are a few bright spots:
— Awareness on the part of a small portion of the population. Solidarity networks are developing everywhere around the environment.
— The associative world continues to develop, especially in the countryside.
— The demonization of psychedelics is underway. Entheogenic plants have been used by various peoples since the dawn of humanity. The main effect of these molecules is the dissolution of the ego. Excess ego in leaders is the worst thing for humanity. Eliminating it is the only solution to avoid the impending catastrophe.

But let's not kid ourselves, we can't avoid it. We know very well that our leaders don't even think about it. They are only concerned about their personal situation, and when it comes to making radical decisions in the collective interest, they won't do it. Or, they'll do it badly and too late.

So, if we want to get through this period, which is approaching ever faster, we must develop a system of operation based on the opposite of our current society. Create or improve horizontal networks and ban all verticality. And this without worrying about the powerful people of this world, who may be settled on Mars or elsewhere.

And then we'll have to rebuild. But we'll talk about that again, maybe later...

7 years on the road

7 years on the road

https://rigveda.blog/

7 years on the road

Table of contents

November 2024..9
On the road. 1967-1968..11
Sahara, here we come..23
The serious stuff begins...39
A short tour of the Maghreb...51
Heading India..59
From Egypt to Sudan...69
From Sudan to Chad..81
Chad and Central African Republic.....................................91
Nigeria - Gabon and a little prison.......................................99
From Cameroon to Morocco..111
Namaste India...121
Next to the Taj Mahal..129
Varanasi, at last!..141
Hardwar, Rishikesh...151
Manali...157
The Kullu small temple...165
A little blonde, a kitten and...171
Degemer mat e Breizh...181
50 years later..185

7 years on the road